EMPOWERING TEAM LEARNING

Enabling ordinary people to do extraordinary things

Michael Pearn

with

Chris Mulrooney, Joan Hodgins, Caroline Lamsdale

INSTITUTE OF PERSONNEL AND DEVELOPMENT

First published in 1998

Design by Paperweight
Typeset by
Fakenham Photosetting Ltd, Fakenham, Norfolk
Printed in Great Britain by
The Cromwell Press, Wiltshire

British Library Cataloguing in Publication Data
A catalogue record for this book is available from the
British Library

ISBN 0-85292-734-7

The views expressed in this book are the authors' own and
may not necessarily reflect those of the IPD

INSTITUTE OF PERSONNEL
AND DEVELOPMENT

IPD House, Camp Road, London SW19 4UX
Tel: 0181 971 9000   Fax: 0181 263 3333
Registered office as above. Registered Charity No. 1038333
A company limited by guarantee. Registered in England No. 2931892

EMPOWERING
TEAM
LEARNING

Michael Pearn is a chartered occupational psychologist with a PhD in psychology. He is a Fellow of the British Psychological Society and of the IPD, as well as a partner in Pearn Kandola, Occupational Psychologists. His other publications for the IPD are (with Rajvinder Kandola) *Job Analysis: A manager's guide* (2nd edn 1993) and (with Chris Mulrooney) *Tools for a Learning Organisation* (1995).

Other titles in the series:

The Institute of Personnel and Development is the leading publisher of books and reports for personnel and training professionals, students, and for all those concerned with the effective management and development of people at work. For details of all our titles, please contact the Publishing Department:
tel. 0181-263 3387
fax 0181-263 3850
e-mail publish@ipd.co.uk
The catalogue of all IPD titles can be viewed on the IPD website:
http://www.ipd.co.uk

CONTENTS

ACKNOWLEDGEMENTS

This book would not have been possible without the commitment and energy of more than 120 empowered team members in eight different organisations.

We would also like to thank our colleagues at Pearn Kandola. Particular thanks go to Johanna Fullerton, Nicole Banerji, Tim Payne, Jasmin Ahmed, and Carol Keane.

Thanks go also to Anne Cordwent at the IPD, and to Christine Hamilton for very helpful editorial advice.

Finally, we would not have been able to produce this book without the hard work and support of Sandra MacLeod, Candy Watts, and Anita Aspill; their efforts and support throughout were greatly appreciated.

Michael Pearn
Chris Mulrooney
Joan Hodgins
Caroline Lamsdale

Dublin and Oxford, June 1998

PREFACE

Why have we written this book?

At the heart of this book lies a belief that in many organisations people have become 'dis-empowered' through learned apathy. They subordinate their intelligence and creativity to others – the people who are *supposedly* in authority over them. Unfortunately, this attitude is compounded by the constraints of organisational structures, policies, and culture.

This book describes a method that enables people who are not usually seen as experts, and who are frequently at the lower levels of the organisational hierarchy, to overcome fear, lack of confidence and a presumed lack of competence. The method enables people to achieve things normally expected of those in expert or superior roles. In addition, the method allows these people to achieve results in a way that can have a lasting effect on the organisation. Because of the way in which the results are achieved, 'empowered team learning' can produce high impact and a commitment to ensuring long-lasting success. Many organisations have found that this is not always the case with expert-led or top-down initiatives. Empowered team learning is a way of bringing about embedded and sustainable change – change that is led from the ground up.

This book is written for HR specialists and line managers who wish to develop a better understanding of the process and what it can achieve. Several detailed case-studies are central to this book, and we hope their inclusion will help readers to see what empowered team learning can achieve in practice. We believe that readers will be able to draw on these case-studies for practical hints and tips, and also gain insight into the powerful way in which empowered team learning enables ordinary people to achieve extraordinary things.

The book describes the key steps of empowered team learning in detail, as well as the key workshops and meetings. Our aim is to provide enough practical guidance and support material to enable readers to design and run an empowered team learning process themselves. We are not, however, seeking to produce 'a practitioner's guide' to teamworking, empowered teams, or teambuilding, and have not attempted to provide guidance on general coaching and facilitation skills. These subjects are important in thinking about teams but are already extensively covered in other books. We believe this book offers a unique method, backed up with supporting materials and practical guidance, which can help to lead change from the ground up.

We know that the method described in this book works because we have seen its results. However, the detail of the process is secondary to the overall aim of motivating a team of people, and progressively building its confidence *and* competence to achieve a result that would normally be assigned to others 'more qualified'. We have been struck by the way in which the results of empowered team learning are often pleasing to the members of the team, who are frequently surprised by their own achievements. Even more striking, though, is the response of the wider organisation or system in which the team operates. Those outside the team are often impressed, and sometimes even amazed, by what the team has achieved.

We hope that you will enjoy the book and be stimulated to try empowered team learning or a variation of it. We recognise that relatively few people will read the book from cover to cover and we hope that the following chapter-by-chapter overview will direct you to the sections most relevant to you.

Chapter-by-chapter overview
Chapter 1 Empowered team learning: the drivers' story

We describe how a team of HGV drivers, concerned that their jobs were under threat, self-managed a project in which they designed and carried out an attitude survey on themselves *without* the involvement of managers or survey experts. They then went on to present a set of conclusions and recommendations on working practices which resulted in significant change in the company.

Chapter 2 How ordinary people can achieve extraordinary things

We introduce the key steps of empowered team learning, look at why it is important and relevant today, and examine the significance of the method. We highlight a range of situations in which we have used empowered team learning to lead change from the ground up.

Chapter 3 Empowered team learning: the method in detail

We describe the method in detail, examining both *why* and *how* it works. There are two sections. The first looks at the distinctive features of empowered team learning; the second at the key steps of empowered team learning.

Chapter 4 Changing hearts and minds to achieve world-class behavioural safety

We present a second detailed case-study describing the story of a team which set out to create a 'safety-first' culture at Europe's only alumina extraction plant. We describe how a group of shop-floor operators and craft-workers self-managed a project to create and bring about behavioural safety *without* the involvement of safety experts or managers, to achieve world-class innovation.

Chapter 5 A step-by-step guide to empowered team learning workshops

We describe the distinctive features of the facilitation process used to bring about empowered team learning. We also describe, *in detail*, the facilitation processes and supporting materials underpinning each of the five workshops that are critical to empowered team learning.

Chapter 6 Empowered team learning case-studies

We describe four shorter case-studies of empowered team learning. In each of them we provide enough detail of the

processes involved to enable a skilled facilitator to replicate them. All four stories draw attention to different
aspects of empowered team learning.

Chapter 7 Managing empowered team learning

We draw on our experiences of empowered team learning to
identify practical hints and tips that could help both potential
sponsors and facilitators of empowered team learning.

Resource Learning in teams

This appendix summarises the literature on how teams learn.

Making the most of this book

We hope the following 'map' will be helpful. It is structured
around the five key questions we anticipate readers may want
to ask of this book, which are:

- [ ] What is empowered team learning?
- [ ] What is special about empowered team learning, and why
does it work?
- [ ] What skills do I need to facilitate empowered team learn-
ing?
- [ ] What can empowered team learning achieve in practice?
- [ ] What are the key issues I need to deal with in putting
empowered team learning into practice?

A suggested 'route' for answers to these questions is given in
Figure 1.

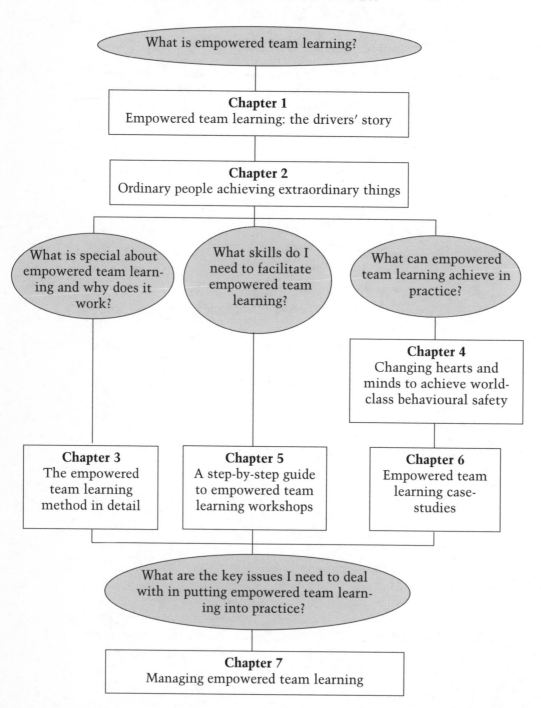

Figure 1
MAKING THE MOST OF THIS BOOK

1 TEAM LEARNING: THE DRIVERS' STORY

The drivers and the situation

We have found that the real power of empowered team learning comes across most strongly when we talk about actual examples. So we begin with one of the two detailed case-studies in this book, recounting the drivers' story as an example of empowered team learning in practice. Later on, we will describe the principles on which empowered team learning is based.

The company was one of the largest oil companies in the UK enjoying a quarter of the market for petroleum products, and it maintained its own directly employed HGV drivers to distribute its products. Five years previously the tanker drivers had numbered over 1,100 and were the second-highest-paid group of manual workers in the country. Since then the company had de-recognised the union, and the number of drivers had fallen to just over 400. New terms and conditions had been introduced, including flexibility agreements and new operating standards.

The 400 drivers were now delivering more product than the 1,100 drivers had five years previously, but they were unhappy and were seen as unco-operative in the face of continuing change. The company wanted to commence a new round of negotiations on further changes in terms and conditions. There was also concern about low morale and about an increase in driver accidents and operational mistakes. Some of the drivers believed that the new operating standards were too tight, although it was widely recognised that they had in the past been negotiated to levels that were far too generous and unsustainable in today's ever more competitive operating environment. They were nervous that the company was going to lay them off and use contract drivers in their place, as had been done by several of the company's competitors.

Neither the management team nor the company's 400 HGV drivers appeared to understand each other.

The management team decided to carry out a consultation with the drivers to find out exactly what they thought about such issues as the operating standards, current terms and conditions, communication between drivers and management, and the possibility of expanding the drivers' role.

A number of attitude surveys had been carried out with the HGV drivers in previous years by external agencies, but somehow the findings had not led to any significant change. The drivers were highly cynical about the surveys, which they saw as attempts at manipulation by management.

The management team decided to consider empowered team learning. A specially formed team of drivers would be progressively equipped with the skills and understanding to design and carry out the consultation for themselves and to present their conclusions to the management team. As a first step, the entire senior management team attended a one-day workshop to examine the idea of empowered team learning and to decide whether to commit to the process with the 400 HGV drivers. The management team needed to be convinced that it was not taking the risk of making an unsatisfactory situation even worse.

The formal objectives of this workshop were:

□ to explore and deepen the senior management team's understanding of the pros and cons of directly employing HGV drivers
□ to identify how the management team could ensure that it really understood the drivers' viewpoint
□ to examine the pros and cons of different ways of obtaining more information
□ to evaluate the pros and cons of allowing the drivers to design and run the consultation process themselves with minimal management involvement.

The design of the workshop did not centre on explaining empowered team learning and presenting it to the management team as the solution to their needs.

The first phase of the workshop was designed to clarify the

management team's thinking on the key issues. This was done by brainstorming several questions:

☐ *What are the possible benefits to the company of having directly-employed drivers?*

☐ *What, if any, are the disadvantages of having directly-employed drivers?*

☐ *In what ways would a directly-employed driver be the same as a contract driver? In what ways different?*

The exercise revealed to the management team the range of thinking that existed within the group itself and emphasised the need to really understand the drivers' own perspective. This was done by brainstorming all the possible benefits of a consultation exercise with the drivers:

> *Think of all the possible reasons for a consultation exercise.*

The actual output of the discussion is shown below:

☐ to build up two-way confidence
☐ to improve morale
☐ to gain a lot of knowledge
☐ to jointly clarify values and perceptions
☐ to save money
☐ to help shape strategy and direction
☐ to achieve a shared instead of imposed outcome
☐ to challenge preconceptions
☐ to convey (and share) a vision
☐ to reinforce commitments to the drivers
☐ to release tension
☐ to improve performance
☐ to benefit from new ideas/innovative thinking
☐ to identify real training/development needs
☐ to reinforce driver identity.

The team then listed all the things that could go wrong, highlighting the dangers of making a bad situation even worse, the risk that the process might be manipulated and distorted, and the possibility that expectations might be raised in a way that could lead only to disappointment. The management team also recognised that it might not like what the drivers had to say. It was also recognised that a failure to get the consultation right would make future attempts even more difficult.

The management team decided in favour of an in-depth consultation that in some way would break the mould from the past. Having listed all the ways in which information could be gathered, the main methods were looked at and the pros and cons of each method were brainstormed. The management team used its own analysis to conclude that face-to-face interviews and focus group discussions with all 400 drivers was the best way forward. The management team's analysis of the pros and cons of using focus groups was:

For	Against
+ dialogue possible	− good process needed
+ involvement of all the drivers	− take too long?
+ research their responses	− summarising process needed
+ probe in depth	− consistency could be a problem
+ flexibility	− skilful group leaders needed
+ comfortable for the drivers	− risk of peer pressure

The next issue to be addressed was that of who should conduct the exercise. The management team brainstormed the pros and cons of giving the responsibility for the consultation to different categories of people (with appropriate levels of support).

☐ the management team itself

☐ the drivers

☐ supervisors

☐ an external contractor

☐ a combination of the above.

The management team decided in favour of allowing the drivers to design and carry out their own consultation. An analysis of the pros and cons is given below:

For	Against
+ high credibility with drivers + acceptability to other drivers + confidence in the process + break with convention + time less critical + open, frank discussions possible + drivers' own language	− loss of control − inconsistency − whom do we select? − data one-sided − more peer group pressure − not really collaborative

By contrast, the arguments for and against the notion that the task should be assigned to an external contractor, as had been the case in the past, were seen as:

For	Against
+ done quicker + technical competence in survey management + likely to be impartial + comparison data	− top management credibility low − low credibility with drivers − preparation time − less understanding of the company, the activity, history − costs − reduced company control − management would learn less − contractors' analysis insufficient on its own − unlikely in itself to improve relations with drivers

The management team decided that they would ask a specially selected project team of HGV drivers to design and run the consultation process. It was decided that a supervisor and a training officer who were trusted and respected by the drivers should also form part of the team. A further decision was made that the consultation exercise would involve all 400 drivers, and be completed within three months, and that the project team was to work on behalf of *all* the drivers.

Communicating with the drivers

The management team communicated its decision to the 400 HGV drivers as follows:

Why we need to consult

There have been many changes in the last few years and our distribution business is now recognised as a professional and efficient operation.

However, we are all aware of areas of safety and operational performance which we must put right to maintain this reputation. It is also important for us to look ahead and see how we can build on our achievements.

We need to work together to understand the problems that are affecting safety and operational performance and drivers' job satisfaction, and to explore ways in which these can be overcome.

We want to work with you to explore how the role of the driver can be developed and to identify what changes we each need to make to increase the quality and security of the in-house operation.

The next phase was to recruit drivers to the project team and take them through the same series of exercises that the management team had been through in the workshop described above. In this way the project team could draw its own conclusions about the value of carrying out the consultation in the manner proposed.

Building the confidence and competence of the project team

When they first arrived at the initial workshop, the eight team members were visibly nervous. This was a new experience for them. They were unused to attending extended workshops in hotels. They did not really know what was expected of them and were fearful of being shown to be ignorant.

The workshop objectives were to:

1   develop a shared understanding of what the workshop was trying to achieve
2   agree how best to carry out the project
3   jointly plan the whole project
4   get skilled up for the task ahead so that it could be approached with confidence
5   think through and plan for what happens next.

The first day of the workshop was entitled *Sharing our thinking* and followed a series of brainstorming sessions identical to those conducted at the management team workshop. This enabled the project team members to clarify and share their own thinking and to commit to the process they had undertaken. They also participated in some practical team learning exercises which provided light relief but also insight into how they could function effectively as a project team. At the end of the first day they had come to realise that they were equal members of the project team, and began to feel excited about the prospect. They had started to overcome their fears that they might not be able to cope. They realised they had a crucial role to play, that the rest of the workshop was designed to equip them with the skills and understanding needed to carry out the task, and that they would receive whatever support they required.

The second day of the workshop was entitled *Planning and skilling up*. It focused on:

- □ brainstorming the options available for gathering information
- □ brainstorming and agreeing on the criteria for choosing between options
- □ choosing the preferred approach and understanding how it would work
- □ identifying what they could hope to get from discussions with their fellow drivers and what should be done to prevent things going wrong
- □ creating a framework for the group discussions and the one-to-one interviews to be conducted
- □ practice sessions with a draft framework
- □ feedback and reviews to revise the framework and create guidelines and standards
- □ reflection on what had been achieved.

The third day was entitled *Consolidation and planning ahead,* and focused on:

- □ brainstorming and deciding how to ensure that the project team obtained reliable and accurate information
- □ syndicate work to agree quality standards for the output from each focus group

□ applying the quality standards in practice sessions with feedback

□ reviewing practical sessions and agreeing on guidelines and support material for focus group leaders

□ reviewing arrangements and logistics

□ planning ahead and preparing for the next workshop at which the collated data from the focus groups would be summarised (before checking back with the drivers)

□ reflecting on what the workshop had achieved.

Preparing for the consultation

A key output from the workshop was a mission statement which is shown below. Part of the importance of this mission statement was that it was created by the team itself, and not imposed upon it. The mission statement was sent to the 400 drivers as part of a briefing to encourage them all to co-operate with the team. The project team saw this as a real opportunity to communicate to management what drivers felt about a number of key issues that affected them and about their relations with the company. Initially the project team felt nervous about its ability to carry out the task in a professional manner, but nevertheless felt excited at the opportunity. They knew they needed to get it right or the chance might not come again.

The project team's mission statement

□ to honestly encourage people to talk to us in an open and relaxed manner about the everyday problems we face in delivering our products

□ to get the drivers to talk to us about such issues as

 i) job satisfaction
 ii) safety
 iii) customer service

and any other issues of concern to them

□ to gather ideas about how the drivers' jobs can be developed.

The project team planned to run 75 focus groups, each facilitated by two members of the team (always with at least one and often two of the driver members of the project acting as facilitators). The structure of the discussions, the actual wording of the questions, all the support material (including hints and tips for running successful focus groups) and the quality checks were created by the project team itself.

The drivers in the project team decided (for themselves) on the help and support they needed. They progressively built up a guidance manual of support material, including tools and checklists, which ensured that the whole project ran smoothly and generated truthful findings that they could confidently present to management. The confidence of the project team grew.

The questions that the project team decided to put to their 400 colleagues are shown below. The guidance manual created by the project team included checklists on opening and closing the focus group discussions, the procedure for conducting the discussions, practical tips from their own experience, the procedure for checking and sending the information to a central point, quality assurance measures, and the hotline support, contacts and materials needed.

The questions posed by the project team to all drivers in the focus group discussions

1 As far as things are now, what are your personal concerns about your job as a driver (or about your job in relation to drivers)? What would you like to see changed or done differently?

2 What are your main concerns for the future?
  What ideas do you have for doing things differently? Think about how the role can be developed.

3 What are the main issues with regard to customers? What would you like to change?

4 What are your main concerns about safety? What ideas do you have for improving safety?

5 What are your views about management and communications? What changes would you like to see?

6 Do you have any other concerns or issues?

The consultation phase

The focus groups were run intensively over a six-week period. The data were summarised on standard forms, lightly edited, subjected to the agreed quality checks, and collated into a dossier for each member of the project team. Once the data had been collated, the project team attended a three-day workshop during which they jointly analysed and interpreted it under the guidance of a facilitator. The team learned how to collate and summarise information and put it through the agreed quality checks. At all times it was emphasised that the members of the team were working as equals and that the output would be presented jointly.

Making sense of the findings

In this phase, the team members' role was to summarise the main findings, and then, and only then, to agree a joint view on the recommendations to be made to the management team.

   The objectives of the workshop were for the members to:

☐ examine and become familiar with all the findings
☐ identify trends and themes
☐ conduct preliminary analysis on the findings
☐ discuss the implications
☐ consider options
☐ make provisional recommendations for discussion.

The structure of the three-day workshop was as follows:

Day one

1 brainstorming the likely issues to emerge
2 group work to examine the data (working in pairs and small groups)
3 reviewing the issues emerging from the data
4 systematically examining the findings
5 brainstorming likely implications
6 reflecting on what had been achieved.

Days two and three

1 analysing the findings
2 agreeing conclusions (ie the main trends in the data under each of the main headings)
3 brainstorming the recommendations
4 agreeing the evaluation criteria and choosing the recommendations
5 preparing for the interim presentation of the findings to the management team.

Presenting the findings

The main findings were presented to senior management by the project team under five main headings, each of which was backed up by actual quotes from the drivers:

☐ job/salary security
☐ time pressures and delays
☐ trust, honesty and openness
☐ retail markets
☐ safety.

The main conclusions were expressed in a concise and dignified way, quite unlike the cynical and sometimes hostile language of preceding years. For example, the conclusion on trust and openness was expressed in these words:

> *Drivers want to be listened to and told the truth by managers who are skilled at dealing with people and have the time to do so.*

On retail markets the overall conclusion was:

> *Problems associated with the customer service centre, delivery site performance by retailers, and site developments are leading to distribution inefficiencies, safety and legal problems.*

Each conclusion was supported by a detailed list of actual problems and some vivid quotes. The management team was impressed with the quality and reasoned nature of the findings. An immediate positive response was made and over the next 24 months many of the drivers' recommendations were implemented. Some were not, but the reasons for that were clearly communicated to the drivers.

The consultation exercise, which the drivers designed and ran by themselves, showed that they could respond with maturity and a professionalism in which they took pride to complex issues in which they had a vested interest. They demonstrated loyalty to the company, a creative capacity, and an ability to grasp complex issues in a way for which they had not always been credited in the past. In many situations this had been obscured by adversarial mind-sets and a tangle of 'them-and-us' thinking and position-taking. The vast majority of the drivers felt that they had never been asked their opinions seriously before, other than through attitude questionnaires that they felt were being imposed upon them. It was also a breakthrough for the management team. Empowered team learning powerfully demonstrated that by trusting and working with, rather than against, groups of employees, better results could be achieved than had been possible in the past. The outcome gave the team the confidence and the desire to work in a collaborative manner on other sensitive issues. The company had taken what it saw as a risk and it had paid off. Two years later the same team of drivers was given the task of running another survey on the driver population to assess the effects of the changes that had been made and to assess the current level of morale.

2   HOW ORDINARY PEOPLE CAN ACHIEVE EXTRAORDINARY THINGS

What is empowered team learning?

Empowered team learning is the name we have given to the method that enables existing or specially formed teams to achieve things that they did not think possible. In a nutshell, it is a method that helps ordinary people to achieve extraordinary results. Empowered team learning is about progressively equipping a team with the confidence and the competence to undertake tasks normally performed by experts. Consider the following examples:

- A team of shop-floor operators achieve world-class innovation in behavioural safety without the direct involvement of safety experts or management.
- A team of unemployed people self-manage a project in which they learn to design and carry out a survey of the needs of local employers and of what unemployed people in the area have to offer.
- A group of supervisors learn to self-manage the process by which they define their future role into the next century and the kind of development they need to help them to succeed in the future.

Empowered team learning does not rely on experts, and does not require experts to run the process. Anyone with a basic repertoire of facilitation skills can design and run an empowered team learning project. The one thing the facilitator does need is the belief that under the right conditions so-called ordinary people can produce better results than the so-called experts. The real power of empowered team learning comes from the fact that solutions 'from the ground' are more likely to be implemented successfully than those that are imposed.

The role of the facilitator in empowered team learning is to progressively develop the confidence and the competence of the team to meet the challenge of finding and implementing their own solutions.

How empowered team learning works

Empowered team learning is built around processes which enable team members to equip themselves with the confidence and competence required to achieve positive results. It also empowers them to take responsibility for implementation. Empowered team learning enables genuine participation. As well as empowering people to take responsibility for decision-making, it equips them with the skills and resources to succeed.

The benefits of participation by employees in the decision-making process have been widely discussed ever since the early work conducted in this area at the Tavistock Institute in the 1950s. These benefits are neatly summarised by Spencer (1989) as falling into three areas: enhanced individual productivity, improved organisational effectiveness, and heightened organisational competitiveness (see Table 1).

Table 1
THE BENEFITS OF PARTICIPATION (SPENCER, 1989)

Enhanced individual productivity	Increased commitment to goals Increased ownership Increased skills Increased self-confidence
Improved organisational effectiveness	Shared vision and alignment Breaking down internal barriers Improved teamwork Improved communication
Heightened corporate competitiveness	Cross-fertilisation of ideas and information Rapid implementation of ideas

The question whether there are any limits on what can be achieved through empowered team learning is an interesting one. The short answer in terms of results is 'probably not'. However, there are of course many assignments for which the conventionally defined experts may still have to be involved, though they should be brought in by the team itself when it is in a position to manage the expert rather than the other way round. When attempting to evaluate the situations in which empowered team learning can best be used, there is of course no simple answer. Consideration must be given to other team-based interventions and to the specific context in which the team operates.

A well-established definition of a team is: 'A team is a small number of people with complementary skills who are committed to a common purpose for which they hold themselves mutually accountable' (Katzenbach and Smith, 1993). There are different types of teams, in different contexts, seeking to achieve different goals. For instance, Hackman (1986) has described seven broad categories of teams:

- □ top management
- □ task forces
- □ professional support groups
- □ performing groups
- □ human service teams
- □ customer service teams
- □ production teams.

Empowered team learning as defined in this book is applicable to any kind of team.

Empowered team learning is not specifically designed to be a teambuilding intervention. It can, however, have that effect, either on specially created project teams or existing teams who use the method to tackle a difficult issue. Empowered team learning is based on teams' tackling real tasks and, in the process, progressively developing the competence to succeed. Empowered team learning integrates the way teams learn with the work they actually do.

A key aspect of effective teamworking is the ability of a team's members to work effectively with one another. Empowered team learning underlies teambuilding and effective teamworking by creating what Peter Senge describes as 'alignment' within the team (Senge, Roberts, Ross, Smith and Kleiner, 1994). As he put it: 'Building alignment is about

enhancing a team's capacity to think and act in new synergistic ways, with full co-ordination, and a sense of unity.'
Empowered team learning is designed to achieve alignment
in this sense, and it does it through creating a shared understanding of the issues surrounding the task at hand.

Group learning needs to be distinguished from team learning. Group learning occurs where people come together and
learn something which can be anything from first aid to
financial planning. The group is not a team because the individuals do not stay together and their later performance is not
dependent on their combined contributions. Group learning
is a necessary ingredient of team learning but is not sufficient
in itself to produce team learning.

An overview of empowered team learning

An existing or specially formed group is assigned a task or
given responsibilities that it would not normally expect.
Members of the team are supported by just-in-time learning
to develop the understanding required at each stage to ensure
success. The approach to learning involves participative
brainstorming which helps the team to develop *its own*
theory or conceptual models. The team is not directly supported by conventionally defined experts or specialists, or
people in a senior management role. The authority of the
team grows from its shared understanding of the issue being
addressed and from the systematic information-gathering
from key stakeholders which is an essential part of empowered team learning.

There are usually 12 steps to empowered team learning,
involving five key workshops:

1   winning organisational commitment to empowered team
    learning
2   forming the project team
3   exploring the issues (*workshop*)
4   planning the information-gathering (*workshop*)
5   collecting the information
6   making sense of the findings (*workshop*)
7   checking back

8   finding a solution (*workshop*)
9   consulting
10 planning the implementation (*workshop*)
11 briefing
12 reviewing and monitoring meetings.

These steps are described in detail in later chapters of this book. For each step example materials are given as well as case-illustrations from a range of organisations, and examples of actual outputs. The aim of this book is to serve as a resource guide on which facilitators can draw to bring about empowered team learning.

Empowered team learning is a method which can be used to help teams take control of their own learning and achieve extraordinary things. A detailed example of empowered team learning was described in Chapter 1. Further examples will be presented later in the book.

Empowered team learning is not an all-embracing solution. It is a tool that demonstrates a different way of enabling teams to achieve results that would normally be the responsibility, or under the control, of specialists and senior managers. It is, however, a powerful tool for bringing about embedded learning and change. In the next chapter we describe the empowered team learning method in more detail.

3 EMPOWERED TEAM LEARNING: THE METHOD IN DETAIL

In this chapter we look at empowered team learning in detail, examining both *why* and *how* it works. There are two sections: the first looks at the nine distinctive features of empowered team learning, the second at key steps to achieving empowered team learning.

The nine distinctive features of empowered team learning

This section looks at the distinguishing features of empowered team learning. It will help both potential facilitators and sponsors of empowered team learning to understand why and how it works.

There are nine distinctive features. They are:

1 challenging tasks or assignments are undertaken by a team
2 responsibility for the outcome lies with the team
3 self-management
4 just-in-time learning
5 extensive use of brainstorming and participative learning
6 experts and specialists are not involved
7 evolved tools and processes
8 information-gathering as the basis for the team's authority
9 break with convention.

1: Challenging tasks or assignments are undertaken by a team

At the heart of empowered team learning is an existing or specially formed group of people who are assigned a task that they would not normally expect to do. This is probably best illustrated by the tasks undertaken by some of the teams with which we have worked. Table 2 shows different groups and their tasks in ten applications of empowered team learning.

The objectives to be achieved must be of critical significance to the key stakeholders represented in the project team.

Table 2
TEN APPLICATIONS OF EMPOWERED TEAM LEARNING

Team	Task
Operators and craftspeople in a refinery	Define and implement an effective way of improving behavioural safety in a high-risk plant which already possesses world-class accreditation for safety standards.
A group of supervisors in a manufacturing plant, some of whom were to be made redundant	Define the role of the 'Supervisors of the Future', create a competency framework and a self-managed development process.
A group of unemployed people registered with a local employment service	Design and carry out a survey of local employment opportunities and match them to the needs of local employers.
Line managers in a food company	Design and implement a self-development process and a performance management system.
Operatives, craftspeople and managers in a refinery	Carry out a survey to define roles and associated competencies for three layers of personnel in a de-layered organisation.
Dealers and chief dealers in a commercial bank	Design and implement a self-managed personal and career development process.
Owner/managers of small businesses (SMEs)	Form a self-managed and self-directed network to become a virtual learning organisation.
A representative cross-section of staff at a new manufacturing unit within an electronics manufacturing plant	Design and implement new ways of working to take advantage of new technology.
A representative cross-section of a company	Identify what needs to change and how to genuinely bring about desired culture change.
A small team of junior HR specialists in a fast-growing and diversifying retail organisation	Create a company-wide strategy on competencies to meet current and possible changes in the business.

2: Responsibility for the outcome lies with the team

The project team is given a clear and specific remit which sets the boundaries for the team's objectives, processes and action plans. Within these boundaries, though, the project team has complete autonomy and takes full responsibility for the outcome.

Although the objectives are often outlined by senior managers, achievement of the objectives is the responsibility of the team. The members of the team know this from the outset. They know that they are being given responsibility for a critical assignment that would normally be given to experts or people who are more senior in the organisation. They recognise that it is an act of trust.

It is therefore important that the members of the team are drawn from the people in the organisation who are most directly affected by the issue being addressed. They should have good reasons to ensure that the outcome is a lasting success.

This was clearly the case with Chapter 1's HGV drivers who realised that they were being given the chance to say directly to management what the issues really were. There were no intermediaries such as unions, survey experts or consultants. Whatever was said was directly attributable to the driver population; the project team therefore realised that they were accountable not only to the management team but also to all 400 HGV drivers.

Giving a team this level of responsibility and trust is motivating to its members, and facilitates effective self-management of the process.

3: Self-management

The project team should be self-managed and, in some cases, self-directed. Ideally it should have no formal leadership and no direct involvement of senior managers. If managers are members of the project team, it is important that they are there as equals and not in a leading role.

By 'self-managed', we mean that the team takes responsibility for the way it operates and what it does within the team's agreed remit. By 'self-directed', we refer to a team which sets or modifies its remit and/or mission, in addition to being self-managed. In some empowered team learning processes, the project team is self-managed – as was the case with the drivers described in Chapter 1. Here, the team was not in a position to change the remit it had been given. We have also worked with project teams which have been self-directing and free to create and/or alter their remit for themselves.

One of the benefits of being self-managed is increased innovation. A number of studies have found that a democratic, participative leadership style encourages group innovation. People need to be responsible for their learning experiences in order for them to be effective (Knowles, 1987).

Much of what is argued for empowered teams is also true of empowered team learning. Wellins , Byham and Wilson (1991) suggest, for example, that people need to be included in the empowerment process at the outset. If managers/supervisors or others assumed traditional 'management' roles, empowered teams would inevitably be blocked in their quest for collective learning. Manz and Sims (1989) suggest that effective leaders in an empowered team environment must be encouraged to learn how to 'lead others to lead themselves'.

Hackman (1986) has identified five common mistakes, or 'tripwires', made by leaders of learning teams:

□ calling the performing unit a team but managing members as individuals
□ falling off the authority balance beam
□ assembling a large group of people, telling them in general terms what needs to be accomplished, and letting them work out the details
□ specifying challenging team objectives, but skimping on organisational supports
□ assuming that members have all the competencies they need to work well as a team.

Although the longer-term goal of empowered team learning is to be self-managing and possibly self-directing, teams usually require skilful facilitation at least initially, and during the key workshops of the empowered team learning method. This is normally done by someone who is not formally a member of the team although it could be done by the team leader if there is one. The facilitation process used in empowered team learning is described in detail in Chapter 5.

The facilitator can help the team by encouraging members to bring their different frames of reference to the fore. Another critical role of the facilitator is to ensure that every member of the team is fully involved in the initial objective- and rule-setting. The empowered team learning workshops will not be successful in promoting empowered team learning unless decisions are taken collectively by consensus (Cunningham, 1994). Ensuring that every member of the team genuinely contributes to, and commits to, the team's ground rules is an important first step in building the team's confidence in a 'new way of working'.

Another role for the facilitator is to reassure the team members in the face of anxiety about meeting the challenging objectives. Campion, Papper and Medsker (1996) have identified a clear relationship between potency – the extent to which team members believe that the team can be effective – and team effectiveness, which can be measured by productivity, satisfaction and manager judgements. The facilitator's role is to help bring about just-in-time learning (which we describe below), and thereby progressively equip the team with the confidence and competence to achieve its challenging task.

4: Just-in-time learning

One of the most important features of empowered team learning is that the team identifies and practises the skills it needs just before they are needed. The skills are not therefore acquired in an abstract or theoretical setting but in the context of the need to make immediate use of them.

The HGV drivers described in Chapter 1 learned the skills of writing open and relevant questions in the context of designing focus group discussions that they themselves were to run. They later learned the skills of collating, coding and summarising data just prior to analysing the output from the focus groups. Later still they learned presentation skills just before making their first ever formal presentation to senior management.

A key advantage of just-in-time learning is that team

members are not overloaded with theory or information that they cannot immediately use or make sense of. Instead, they deal only with the pertinent skills and understanding required to ensure high-quality results for the next stage of the project. Thompson and Zondlo (1995) captured this principle succinctly: 'Integrating team learning with real-time organisational issues and opportunities enhances both the meaningfulness of the lessons and the quality of the results. Just-in-time learning addresses an immediate need but its lessons create a cascading effect that carries over into longer-term needs.'

Just-in-time learning is important because

□ The team usually needs to gain the confidence gradually over a period of time that it can undertake the task successfully.

□ Input by 'experts', especially at the outset, will overload the team, cause confusion, undermine confidence and create dependency.

□ The team takes charge of its own learning process, making it highly focused and relevant to its evolving needs.

□ The team feels that it is in control and will not yield responsibility to others.

□ The gradual deepening of shared understanding and the development of team members' skills is intrinsically motivating.

5: Extensive use of brainstorming and participative learning

The development of deepened and shared understanding relies heavily on structured brainstorming with virtually no involvement of conventionally defined experts or specialists. This is a very important feature of empowered team learning. Structured brainstorming is used by the team to

□ create an ethos of functioning as a group of equals
□ develop its own thinking
□ create the mission or agreed objectives for the team
□ agree quality assurance standards
□ plan action

☐ agree what data and/or information is needed
☐ identify the relevant sources of information
☐ choose and design the information-gathering methods
☐ interpret information
☐ identify and agree performance indicators
☐ evaluate outcomes
☐ draw conclusions
☐ make recommendations
☐ plan and run presentations to others.

Structured brainstorming initially requires skilled facilitation from a neutral facilitator whose skills partly lie in identifying and wording the questions to be brainstormed by the group (further guidance on the questions to use and the process for facilitating the group can be found in Chapter 5). The facilitator should not be, or seek to function as, an expert leading the group either formally or informally.

6: Experts and specialists are not involved

Considerable emphasis in empowered team learning is placed on utilising the shared knowledge and wisdom available within the team and as a result of systematic surveys and audits designed and carried out by the team itself. The focus of empowered team learning is on helping the team to develop its own theory or conceptual models, using the learning spiral process described below.

The team's systematic data-gathering, which is one of the key stages of empowered team learning, gives the team its prime source of authority. The rigour and objectivity of the information-gathering, combined with the team's gradual evolution of deepened and shared understanding, gives the team considerable credibility and potential to influence its key stakeholders. The language used and the way in which the issues are captured and presented make the team's conclusions more meaningful than the advice of 'experts'. This also gives the team considerable authority in the eyes of the stakeholders it represents.

In empowered team learning, experts are seen as potential

blocks to effective team learning. Organisations tend to use experts when they

- are not confident that they can find a solution for themselves
- believe that experts will protect them from making mistakes
- think experts know things they do not
- need solutions to difficult issues.

Empowered team learning minimises dependency on subject-matter 'experts' and conventional team leadership. Expertise and formal leadership are secondary to the shared understanding and commitment of the team. Empowered team learning substitutes the experts (or leaders) with the team's own acquired authority. Dependency on experts, on the other hand, can reduce the sense of ownership felt by those involved. Issues and solutions are often proposed in ways that feel imposed and do not fit naturally with the experience of the team or the wider stakeholders. Understanding can also be reduced because experts often use language apprehended as jargon.

Some of the disadvantages associated with the use of experts are that they

- are hard to challenge
- do not always respond well to having their opinions challenged by others
- use well-worn criteria and models that are not tailor-made for the particular situation
- are often guided by criteria and needs quite different from those to whom they are giving advice
- often make assumptions and take levels of understanding and/or acceptance for granted, without stopping to check
- often have less impact than might be expected because their involvement inhibits or actively discourages people and groups from thinking for themselves.

7: *Evolved tools and processes*

A prime feature of empowered team learning is the emphasis on the team's developing its own theory or conceptual models. This helps reduce the dependency on experts. Any theory, or set of guiding principles, needed is usually worked out by the project team itself, together with any models, frameworks or working tools using the learning spiral.

The learning spiral (see Figure 2) enables the team to build meaningful conceptual models by drawing on experience, and making this explicit.

There are five key stages in the learning spiral. First, the team members do something. It can be anything – take a decision, some form of action, or something familiar – but done in a different way. Examples might include trying to persuade through negotiation or trying out focus group facilitation skills. The second step is to reflect as a group on how it went and, where possible, obtain feedback from others (eg on what went well, what mistakes were made, and how these mistakes occurred). The third stage is for the team to build a simple model of how to do it better next time, based on its mistakes and experience. This model can take different forms: possibilities include checklists, diagrams, flowcharts and mnemonics. The challenge is to try to capture the team's experience and any lessons learned in terms that are appropriate to it. In effect, the team members are writing advice to themselves about how to do something. The process works best if the facilitator avoids (or ignores) theoretical input at the outset.

The fourth stage involves trying out the task again, but this time doing it with the support of the team's new model. The team then (stage five) reflects on how well it went, obtains feedback where possible, and revises the model in the light of new mistakes and experience. It may be helpful at this stage, but only at this stage, to seek more 'expert' advice on the team's model by additional reading and showing it to others. However, nothing should be included which does not make sense to the team in the light of experience. The reason the process is a spiral rather than a loop is that testing and revising are continuous activities, all the time increasing team members' skill and understanding.

Figure 2
THE LEARNING SPIRAL

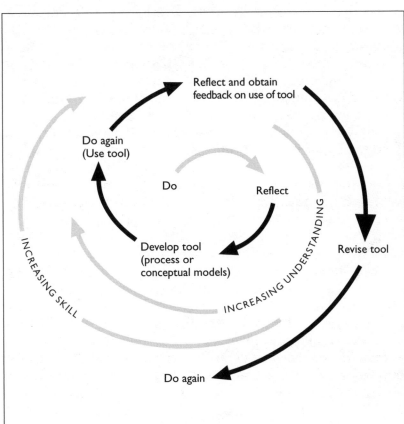

There are two main strands in the learning spiral. The first is related to increasing understanding (by helping the team to build its own theory or guiding principles) and the second to increasing skill in doing or achieving something. Learning begins with developing an understanding of the task in hand, and skill in carrying it out is built on this understanding. Eventually the two overlap, and then the two spiral outwards, with one or the other taking prominence as required.

A key feature of the learning spiral is the expectation that things need not be done or understood perfectly. Errors and mistakes are essential to the achievement of effective learning.

Through reflecting on these mistakes and building them into an 'advisory' model which is continually revised in the light of experience, the spiral optimises learning from mistakes *and* successes. This is important because fear of making mistakes can inhibit learning. In empowered team learning, mistakes are considered not as failures but as important parts of the learning process. Crossan, Djurfeldt, Lane and White (1994) make the powerful point that some learning must result in failure for further learning to occur. The critical role played by mistakes in effective learning is the central theme of our book *Ending the Blame Culture* (Pearn, Mulrooney and Payne 1998).

The advice a team develops for itself using the learning spiral will be much more powerful than any other model or theory offered by experts, however sophisticated and elaborate. Because the team creates a model in its own words, based on its own conclusions and drawn from its own experience, the team achieves what we have called *internalised* or *deep learning*. This is in contrast to the *surface learning* that is often the result of lectures and more traditional teaching methods typical of so much training.

Another example of evolved rather than imposed model-building is described in detail in Chapter 4. Here a group of refinery operators and craftspeople build a complex model of the inter-relationships between behavioural and environmental safety factors. The purpose is to understand the sustained levels of risk-taking and hazard tolerance in an environment which already meets world-class standards of safety. Having built their own complex model, the team then has the understanding and confidence to discard it in favour of a stunningly simple approach to behavioural safety which it knows it can make work.

8: Information-gathering as the basis for the team's authority

Another key feature of empowered team learning is that the team learns how to design and carry out some form of systematic information-gathering to high professional standards. The project team establishes its authority from a deepened and shared understanding of the issues which it gains through the empowered team learning process itself and through the information obtained from key stakeholders. It is critical that the project team bases all its conclusions on information obtained and not solely on its own deliberations and thinking. At this stage, the project team's role is to summarise and capture the views of the large population it represents. It is not to put across its own views. This information-gathering process gives authority to the project team's decisions because it is transparent, participative and democratic.

The project team described in Chapter 1 carried out focus group discussions with 400 HGV drivers. Other empowered learning teams have extended their information-gathering to senior managers, to other companies, the whole organisation, suppliers, customers and other stakeholders. It is a feature of empowered team learning that the team itself decides whose viewpoints are relevant and how they should be assessed.

In all the cases of empowered team learning described in this book the teams learned to identify information needs, and then plan and carry out the data-gathering process, before they learned to summarise the data obtained. In some cases the team checked back with people from whom the information was gathered that its summary was accurate and relevant before proceeding to the next stage – drawing conclusions and making recommendations.

The data gathered, and the insights and lessons that arise as a result, are the basis of the team's decision-making and planning. The information-gathering process is critical because it provides the authority for the project team's recommendations and implementation plans.

9: Break with convention

An important feature of empowered team learning is a break with convention. Empowered team learning is a different way of working. It is based on trust and the belief that ordinary people, given real responsibility and equipped progressively to handle an assignment, will deliver remarkable results. They will have a level of commitment that is relatively rare in traditional centralised hierarchical organisations.

Empowered team learning is the difference:

between…	and…
☐ bringing in specialists to carry out an attitude survey which has only limited impact on the organisation	☐ forming a task group of the target population to design, execute and interpret the survey for themselves, and to make and implement recommendations
☐ asking consultants to design and install a performance management system	☐ empowering a group of middle managers to design and implement a process for the company that they know will really work
☐ inviting safety experts to lead a project team to achieve high standards of behavioural safety	☐ equipping the people who work in a dangerous environment to work it out and implement changes for themselves
☐ senior management's leading a top-down process by which the values of the organisation are defined and developed in detail before being communicated	☐ a co-creation process among equals who are all stakeholders to jointly create an outcome that has the commitment of everyone
☐ senior managers' creating a strategy for change which they then have to sell upwards, outwards, and downwards	☐ empowering a team to consult all the stakeholders and use the information to create a strategy they then have to implement
☐ bringing in specialists to recommend how working practices should be changed to meet the needs of improved manufacturing technology	☐ equipping and supporting the people who work there to work it out and make the changes for themselves.

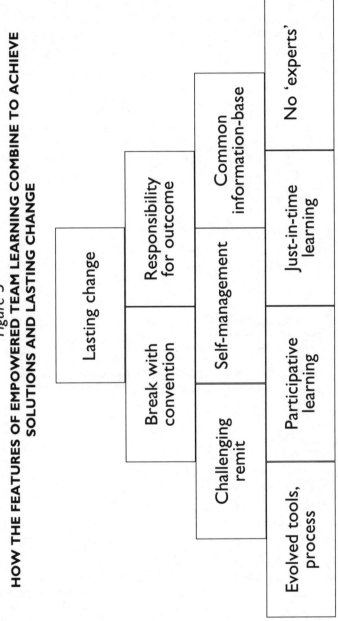

Figure 3
HOW THE FEATURES OF EMPOWERED TEAM LEARNING COMBINE TO ACHIEVE SOLUTIONS AND LASTING CHANGE

One of the key benefits of empowered team learning is that there is often a change in perception, especially among senior managers, about non-specialists and people lower down the formal organisational hierarchy. It becomes apparent that they can not only be trusted to self-manage a process without specialist help but can also produce quality results that have wide acceptance and become embedded in the organisation. Empowered team learning is in a tradition of employee involvement and participation (see Semler, 1993) and is based heavily on our approach to group and organisational learning described in Pearn, Roderick and Mulrooney (1995). The combined effects of the main features of empowered team learning in achieving embedded change is shown in Figure 3.

The 12 key steps of empowered team learning

In its fullest form, empowered team learning has 12 distinct steps (see Figure 4). Five of the steps are workshops which vary in length from one to three days. In some cases the workshops can be combined, as later examples will show, but they are all run in a manner designed to progressively build the project team's confidence and competence to carry out a challenging task.

The structure of the key steps helps the project team to see that the issues it faces can be successfully resolved. In turn, this progressively builds a strong sense of ownership and commitment.

Step 1: Winning organisational commitment

The first step of empowered team learning generally does not involve a team at all. Prior to team establishment, meetings are held with those who are sponsoring the project to ensure that they have a clear comprehension of what empowered team learning entails. The benefits of the approach are outlined at this stage, as are the responsibilities of the organisation to ensure that the process can be a success and lead to embedded change.

To ensure that empowered team learning works well, the project sponsor must consider:

Figure 4
KEY STEPS OF EMPOWERED TEAM LEARNING

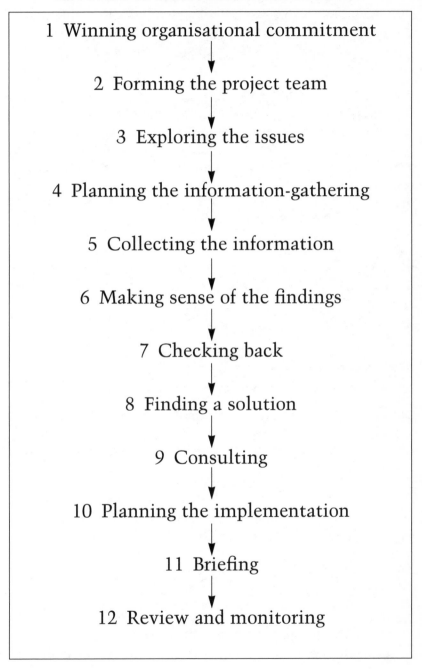

1 Winning organisational commitment

2 Forming the project team

3 Exploring the issues

4 Planning the information-gathering

5 Collecting the information

6 Making sense of the findings

7 Checking back

8 Finding a solution

9 Consulting

10 Planning the implementation

11 Briefing

12 Review and monitoring

- □ how to manage the overall process from concept to implementation
- □ how to provide organisational support where required
- □ how to communicate the objectives and method
- □ how to eliminate potential blocks or barriers to a successful outcome.

Looking back at Chapter 1's example of the HGV drivers, all these issues were considered informally in discussion prior to commitment to the empowered team learning process. Full commitment to the break with convention was made during a workshop with the whole management team. During this workshop the management team systematically examined the issues and experienced some of the methods of the empowered team learning process.

Step 2: Forming the project team

In some cases the team may already be in existence. This is not a problem as long as its members meet the main empowered team learning criteria. These are:

- □ representativeness of the key stakeholders
- □ credibility with those outside the project team
- □ ability to meet time commitments
- □ composition of ideally between six and 10 people.

Alternatively, a team may be specially created for the purpose of empowered team learning. An overarching requirement of a successful team is that its members develop a commitment to the team's goals.

Dechant, Marsick and Kasl (1993) have described team learning in terms of a cyclical model, outlining each stage a team must pass through when moving towards synergistic learning. The four stages of their model are:

- □ *fragmented learning* – where learning has not moved beyond the individual and is inhibited because members hold different frames or mind-sets
- □ *pooled learning* – where clusters of individuals learn within the group, but there is little collective reframing
- □ *synergistic learning* – where meaning schemes are altered

or discarded as a result of collective reframing among group members

□ *continuous learning* – where all team learning processes are used easily and regularly. Collective reframing has become the norm. Members' perspectives are easily integrated and evolved into consensual understanding. The group has developed the habit of seeking out and valuing diversity, internally and externally, in order to broaden its perspective. The team experiments, often – individually and collectively – within the larger organisation, thus extending learning to others.

Empowered team learning, however, is specifically designed to enable synergistic learning to occur very early in a project team's development.

Research also suggests that group cohesiveness can have two contradictory influences on collective learning. Cohesiveness can encourage innovation because it helps team members feel comfortable with the rest of the team. It is reinforced when members of a team are similar to one another. But a high level of similarity can work against innovation. People in homogeneous groups are unlikely to question group decisions, and may focus on relationships rather than tasks. This can potentially lead to the 'group-think' phenomenon (Janis, 1982). Low cohesiveness may be beneficial early in the process of producing creative ideas, and high cohesiveness may help groups to implement innovations successfully. Empowered team learning is specially designed to increase group cohesiveness – but at the same time it increases team members' skills of dialogue and challenge.

The skills which project team members bring with them into the team environment can either facilitate or hinder collective learning. Empowered team learning ensures that the skills of the team are well balanced across its members because all members of the team develop the skills and tools required.

Wellins *et al* (1991) and Danau and Sommerlad (1996) both identify the following competencies as being necessary for effective empowered team working:

□ team, interactive, interpersonal and communication competencies, such as providing others with accurate and complete information, changing position when others offer convincing data, handling conflict and influencing others

☐ action, problem-solving and decision-making skills, such as identifying improvement opportunities and developing and selecting solutions

☐ technical, functional or job competencies, such as in equipment operation and production processes.

All these competencies are developed through empowered team learning. The consequence is that choice of team members in empowered team learning is not a critical issue if the empowered team learning process is adhered to. Credibility and representativeness of stakeholder group is more important when choosing team members.

Step 3: Exploring the issues (Workshop A)

Adult learning theory proposes that once adults see a reason to learn, they will participate actively and creatively in the learning experience. Ungar and Lorscheider (1996) have further suggested that there is a hierarchy of motivation for learning in groups:

☐ being allowed

☐ knowing *how*

☐ knowing *why*

☐ wanting.

The overall aim of the exploratory workshop is to progressively meet each of these four conditions. Although the project team will have been established to accomplish a specific organisational task, the way in which this task is to be carried out is decided by the team itself. In the exploratory workshop, the team therefore creates its own mission statement and sets its own objectives; it establishes the specific goals it is setting itself, and often the strategy and time by which these goals will be achieved. Critically, it also agrees the standard processes and 'ground rules' by which it will work.

In setting its own objectives the team assumes complete responsibility for the outcome of its work. Indeed, the objectives set by the team will focus attention on the learning needs of its members in terms of the skills needed. These skills are then more likely to be learned effectively because they are clearly related to the learners' ability to perform their subsequent work in a better way. The organisational support that will be required in terms of training and/or resources can also be identified at this early stage.

Step 4: Planning the information-gathering (Workshop B)

This workshop is sometimes combined with Workshop A. Here, the project team decides what kind of information it needs and from whom it should get it. It decides on the questions it wants to ask, and practises the skills of asking questions and recording the answers. It also decides on the methods to be used (eg individual interviews, group discussions or questionnaires). Finally, the project team plans the logistics of the data-gathering process and agrees its own quality indicators for the data to be collected and for the remaining stages of the project.

After this workshop the team starts the programme of data-gathering on a trial basis. It then meets to review the effectiveness of the trial at a special review meeting, before commencing the final data-gathering process.

Step 5: Collecting the information

The fifth step of empowered team learning generally involves the team's gathering the information, using the methods it has evolved and practised. The project team has developed the skills needed for this stage and therefore aims to be completely self-sufficient in the information-gathering process.

In order to maintain this self-sufficiency, the team holds interim review meetings during the information-gathering to check on progress and exchange experiences. Changes are made to the information-gathering process in the light of experience, and improvements made to the guidance material created at the planning and preparation workshop.

The interim review meetings are also used to ensure that the information being gathered is collated consistently and on an ongoing basis. The aim is to draw together the information collected into a manageable form without summarising or interpreting it in any way before the project team meets for Step 6.

Step 6: Making sense of the findings (Workshop C)

The project team is taken step-by-step through a series of exercises (see Chapter 5) which enable its members to learn the skills of summarising and classifying data as they systematically work through the information. At this stage the project team does not attempt to interpret the findings or draw conclusions. The focus is entirely on summarising the findings and drawing them together in a manageable framework that can be presented to the people from whom the data was gathered.

Step 7: Checking back

Before progressing any further, the project team presents the summarised findings back to the people from whom the information was gathered. They are specifically asked

☐ Have we captured what you were saying to us?
☐ Does this make sense to you?
☐ Have we missed anything?

Any feedback or comments from them are noted.

Step 8: Finding a solution (Workshop D)

The project team meets again to distill all the information collected, including any feedback obtained during the checking-back process. The aim is to agree a detailed specification for an outcome that would meet the needs of the people who provided the information. The extent to which the project team is representative of the project stakeholders is critical, as is their endorsement of the summarised findings. The project team creates a specification in some detail before planning a consultation process.

Step 9: Consulting

This consultation serves two purposes. First, it checks out the feasibility of the proposals. Second, it secures stakeholders' support. Having agreed a detailed specification, the project team members run group briefing sessions with key stakeholders. Participants are reminded that the information was obtained from them, and the specification is essentially their framework. They are then asked to help improve the specification and to finalise it. In keeping with the empowered team learning approach, the project team takes care in the design of the briefing sessions to allow others to think through the issues for themselves. In this way the project team encourages others to draw their own conclusions rather than simply presenting its thinking to them.

Step 10: Planning the implementation (Workshop E)

At the implementation workshop, the project team draws on the outputs and feedback from the briefing and a meeting with the project sponsor to finalise the specification. The team then uses its final sessions to plan how to bring about changes in the behaviour and attitudes of key stakeholders. It also discusses and plans how to progressively self-monitor. This is important because

□ it enables the team members to recommend agreed solutions to issues/problems that directly affect them and those they represent

□ the project sponsor can use the facts/data provided to gain organisational support for the team's recommendations.

Step 11: Briefing

The team designs and carries out appropriate briefings.

Step 12: Review and monitoring

The team meets on a regular basis to review and monitor progress against the previously identified and agreed indicators for success, and to propose further changes.

In this chapter we have examined empowered team learning in detail, and we have discussed both *why* and *how* it works. In the first section we looked at the nine distinctive features of empowered team learning. In the second we outlined the 12 key steps of empowered team learning. We started this book with the drivers' story. That was an example of empowered team learning in practice. In the next chapter we tell the story of a team of shop-floor operators and craft workers in terms of the 12 key steps of empowered team learning.

4 CHANGING HEARTS AND MINDS TO ACHIEVE WORLD-CLASS BEHAVIOURAL SAFETY

Empowered team learning in key-step-by-key-step action

Empowered team learning proved to be a critical factor in creating a 'safety-first' culture at Europe's only alumina extraction plant. A group of shop-floor operators and craft workers self-managed a project to create and bring about their own self-defined concept of behavioural safety without the involvement of safety experts or managers. This story demonstrates how empowered team learning can help to achieve world-class innovation. We tell this story in some detail in order to provide readers with real insight into how the empowered team learning method works in practice.

Step 1: Winning organisational commitment

The refinery occupies a site which cost £650 million to build in the late 1980s, and currently employs 420 people. Great emphasis is placed on safety, and the company safety record is world-class. In fact, the company has achieved the internationally recognised ISRS accreditation, which is equivalent to the ISO 9000 standard.

The company was committed to maintaining a zero-accident-and-injury culture. At the time of the project it was recognised that this could only be achieved if the behaviour and thinking of everyone on the site resulted from a safety mind-set in addition to adherence to the safety systems, procedures and processes already in place. This prompted a safety strategy aimed at developing a culture in which everyone always thinks and acts in a safe manner. The strategy commenced in January 1996 and was self-managed by a project team of volunteers from the shop-floor and craft sections. The team successfully brought about changes in attitudes and behaviour in everyone they worked with. As a result, there were measurable improvements in safety.

The overriding aim of the project was that behavioural safety should be established, implemented and evaluated by the people most affected by the outcome – that is, the operators and craftspeople, and not their managers or safety experts.

Empowered team learning enabled the team to develop the confidence and the skills to self-manage the project. Pat Sweeney, the human resources manager, explains the difference that empowered team learning made to the end result:

> Because the group made its own choices and decisions, and arrived at its own conclusions, there was not only a greater sense of responsibility but also a keen desire to succeed. Response to the group's surveys amongst its fellow workers and management is particularly interesting. The type and detail of information obtained suggests a high level of trust and openness has been achieved across the entire workforce.

Step 2: Forming the project team

A project team was set up comprising eight volunteers to work on behalf of their peers. The team consisted of five operators, one fitter, one instrument/electrical craftsperson, and one team facilitator. The team was representative in a highly credible way of the people who would be most directly affected by the outcome of the project – those who worked in the most dangerous part of the plant. The team was assisted by one of the authors, whose role was to guide its members through each step and to support them in the achievement of the project aims – but *not* to lead them.

Step 3: Exploring the issues

The eight volunteers received a briefing on the aims of the project. The key purpose of the exploratory workshop was to begin the process of deepening team members' shared understanding and developing their ownership of the project aims. The objectives were to

□ develop a shared understanding of the project aims

□ clarify the role of the project team
□ define objectives
□ map out the main stages of the project
□ identify performance and success indicators
□ agree an action plan and timetable.

The meeting began with brief introductions. The facilitator explained that his role was to facilitate and support the team in the achievement of its project aims, but not to lead it.

Through a series of facilitated brainstorming sessions, the team decided how it wanted to run the project. As a result of these discussions the team began to realise that it really was in charge of the project. It also recognised that full commitment from every member of the team would be needed to make the project work.

One of the key objectives, as outlined above, was to develop a shared understanding of the project. Instead of arranging a formal presentation on the project, the facilitator suggested that the team members pool their thoughts and knowledge on this topic using brainstorming techniques. The questions considered by the team were:

□ *Based on what you already know about the project, what words or phrases come to mind?*
□ *How would you like this project to be different from other projects you have experienced? In what ways would you like it to be similar?*

Some of the distinguishing features of this project emphasised by the team included the self-managed and self-directed nature of the work to be conducted. It was recognised that the project would be driven by the team itself and would not be controlled by others.

As one of the team members (Mark Sheehan) commented on completion of the project,

> This project made those involved feel it was theirs, so you had a group of people who were safety-conscious, rather than just safety officers. We only got support from management when we asked for it. It was set up and run by the people on the floor. People grew up to safety – ie people accepted being challenged

on safety issues and did not take it personally. There was less paperwork, more dialogue and action.

The next step was to clarify the project objectives and capture them in a mission statement created jointly and agreed by all members of the team. The team brainstormed the characteristics of a good mission statement, rank-ordered the preferred criteria, and eventually agreed on the mission statement shown below:

Our mission is to achieve:

1 An accident-free site through changing our own behaviour and a climate that supports a safety-first approach.

2 A safety-first mind-set developed by the people it affects.

3 Climate and circumstances in which everyone adopts a safety-first mind-set.

We will do this by:

1 Working as a team.
2 Gathering information on actual practice.
3 Trying new approaches.
4 Closely involving everyone in the pilot site.
5 Learning from others.
6 Creating and piloting a way of developing a life-long safety-first approach.

A number of brainstorming questions were then used to draw out the team's ideas for a project plan. These included:

- *What are the possible benefits of developing a project plan?*
- *How can we tell if we are being successful?*
- *What must we take into account to ensure we are successful?*
- *In carrying out this project what could go wrong?*

The facilitator assisted the team in putting together an action plan in the light of the items that were raised by team members in response to these brainstorming questions. The key phases of the action plan were highlighted as:

1 prepare the project team
2 brief the people in the area
3 design and carry out an audit
4 interpret the information/data
5 draw conclusions and feedback
6 design the intervention to change mind-sets and achieve behavioural safety
7 implement the pilot scheme
8 evaluate and revise the scheme in the light of experience
9 pilot again
10 evaluate
11 go site-wide.

A key feature of this project was that the team members worked on behalf of their peers. The team stayed very close to its constituency, involving them at all key stages. It gathered data from them, summarised outcomes, briefed, consulted, obtained ideas and suggestions, and generally worked towards the achievement of ownership at every stage and by everyone involved.

Step 4: Planning the information-gathering

At the same workshop the team members began to prepare for the task of gathering information from their peers. They brainstormed the issues they would be interested in asking their peers about in relation to personal risk-taking behaviour and improving safety. The team decided to use two information-gathering methods: small group discussions, and interviews in pairs.

The team planned the information-gathering process in detail at a separate two-day planning workshop. The objectives were to:

☐ review the outputs of the previous meeting
☐ agree the questions to be asked in the audit

- plan the information-gathering in detail
- practise asking the proposed questions and recording the answers
- think ahead to later phases in the project
- agree the performance measures for the project.

The team members considered what could go wrong during the process and suggested ways in which potential problems could be overcome.

Some of the team's concerns included

- interviewer factors (eg interview domination by the interviewer, problems in remembering the information gathered, etc)
- interviewee factors (eg refusal to respond, mistrust, etc)
- situational factors (eg noise, distractions, interruptions, etc).

The output of the brainstorming sessions was used to develop guidelines for the team. It was also used to plan the information-gathering so as to maximise the quality and reliability of the information obtained.

The team created its own checklist for introducing and closing an interview to ensure consistency. A significant amount of time was spent by the project team members in practising the questions on each other, and the process was refined in the light of this experience. In effect, the team pooled its thinking and practical experience to write advice to itself about how to interview peers in a highly personalised way.

The questions the project team members planned to ask everyone who worked in their area are shown below:

Section I	Your views
a)	For you personally, what works well in keeping you healthy and safe?
b)	Which ones (three) are most important to you personally? Why?
c)	What, else would make a difference?
d)	What, in your view, does not work well?
e)	Which of these bad things is most important to you?
f)	Why doesn't it work? What is wrong?

Section 2   Risk-taking

a)   When are you most likely to take a chance and risk getting
                    injured?

b)   Why do you think people leave things unsafe or do things
                    unsafely?

c)   How do you assess risk?

Section 3   Your own experiences

a)   Can you recall a recent specific instance when you knowingly
                    acted unsafely? Describe the circumstances.

b)   What things do you occasionally do which could result in an acci-
                    dent?

c)   Would you use or have you ever used a 'refuse-to-work policy'?
                    Why?

Section 4   Improving safety

If you could change one thing in

a)   the area you work in

b)   your colleagues

c)   yourself

what would it be?

Step 5: Collecting the information

An interim review meeting was held during the information-gathering stage. This was an opportunity for the team to check on progress and make changes to the information-gathering materials and process in the light of experience. The objectives of this meeting were to

□ review the progress of the project

□ discuss any feedback from the company safety meetings

□ review how the interviews were going, and in particular, the nature of the information being obtained, practical issues around the wording of questions, timing, structure, and skills needs

□ review the project timetable

□ plan the remaining interviews

□ review what should happen next.

The meeting began with the participants' stating how they

perceived the information-gathering to be going. Problems or concerns were discussed and addressed in a supportive manner, the team members drawing on each others' experience to find solutions. In the light of their discussions, the team made the following decisions:

☐ to allow the interview to flow (average time between 45 and 75 minutes)

☐ to allow people to get things off their chests

☐ to give a summary of types of questions – one page, key phases, etc – on the day of the interview

☐ to show each question in writing when asking it

☐ to make changes to the wording of some of the questions and to the introduction.

A complete dossier of all the information gathered by the team was created, and each team member was given a copy to work on at the next workshop.

Step 6: Making sense of the findings

All summarising and classifying of the data was carried out by the team jointly at a three-day workshop. The project team learned the skills of summarising and coding information, and systematically worked through the data using a clustering process to make sense of the findings. The key objectives of the workshop were to

☐ review how well the information-gathering had gone

☐ identify the main themes that emerged

☐ learn how to summarise and code the information collected

☐ plan how to summarise the findings back to the people interviewed.

Making sense of the information collected was an intensive process. The hard work of analysing the information was interspersed with several practical team activities to provide breaks and light relief. These included a knot-tying exercise and a ball-throwing exercise. As well as being fun to do, these exercises also helped the team to develop insight into team learning. The lessons learned could then be applied during the workshop and, indeed, during the course of the team's everyday work.

The workshop began with the team's brainstorming the key issues and trends that they remembered from the interviews they had conducted before any in-depth analysis of the actual data was carried out. The team then created a plan for tackling the rest of the information. As the workshop progressed, the team gained the expertise and confidence to work with larger chunks of the data. Furthermore, with practice and periodic reviews, a high level of consistency in coding the information was achieved. This consistency enabled the team to work in small groups on different interviews, and therefore resulted in speedier data analysis.

The team decided to run briefing sessions with everyone interviewed and to summarise back the findings to them. The workshop therefore concluded by planning this checking-back process.

Step 7: Checking back

The team members summarised and presented the findings of the information-gathering back to the people who had been interviewed or taken part in group discussions. The sessions were run by members of the project team, working in twos and threes, and followed the structure agreed at the previous workshop:

1 things that work well
2 things that do not work well
3 why people take risks
4 your list of unsafe conditions/practices, comments on a refuse-to-work policy
5 what people feel they need to learn
6 what people feel needs to change.

At the end of the sessions, the team members invited comments from their peers and asked the following questions:

☐ *What are your reactions to this summary?*
☐ *Does it look accurate and realistic to you?*

□ *What advice or ideas do you have to offer? After all, this project is about your safety and that of everyone on site.*

All feedback was recorded by the team, with a view to analysing it and incorporating it into their thinking and planning for later stages of the project.

Step 8: *Finding a solution*

The project team took part in a two-day workshop to distill all the information collected and the feedback from the checking-back sessions. The main aim was to identify those behaviours which would actually make a difference to employees' personal safety. The objectives were to

□ review feedback from the summarising-back sessions

□ decide what needed to change to help bring about higher standards of behavioural safety

□ decide what people needed to learn to help them acquire a safety-first frame of mind

□ specify how the changes in behaviour and attitude were best learned.

The workshop began with the team members' spending a few minutes quietly reviewing and making notes of the main points they saw coming out of the checking-back sessions. These points were shared and recorded by the facilitator on a flipchart. The team members then worked in pairs to brainstorm the possible factors in their environment that could contribute to an explanation of continuing risk of accidents on site. The framework used to capture the team's views is presented as Table 3. The exercise was repeated again, this time focusing on behaviours. The aim was to produce a set of behavioural and non-behavioural factors, many of which were interlinked, affecting safety. These were then used by the project team to explain, with reference to the interconnections between factors, why the risk of accidents persisted on site.

The eventual diagram created by the team to show the complex interplay of factors is presented in Figure 5.

Table 3
WHY UNSAFE CONDITIONS CONTINUE

Step one: Identify the main components that contribute to unsafe conditions. Some of them are listed below.

Poor design/access

Non-adherence to procedures

Unsafe practices

Any more?

Step two: Identify the main behaviours/attitudes that make things worse. Some of them are listed below.

A habit of non-intervention

Cynicism: why bother?

'It won't happen to me'

Any more?

Figure 5
THE EXPLORATORY DIAGRAM PRODUCED BY THE PROJECT TEAM TO EXPLAIN THE PERSISTENCE OF HAZARDS

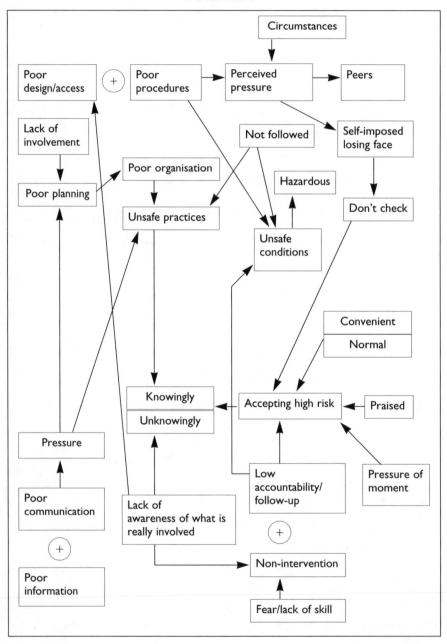

The facilitator then asked the team to brainstorm the enablers (ie the factors already helping to secure behavioural change) and the blockers (ie the obstacles that could be blocking or interfering with the change). The key questions discussed by the team included:

□ *What needs to change? When deciding what to focus on, what things should we take into account?*

□ *What do we consider are the main priorities?*

□ *If we want these things to change, what are the enablers and what are the potential blockers?*

The project team then discussed what needed to be done differently by everyone across the site in order to achieve total commitment to behavioural safety. The key themes that emerged from the discussion included:

□ improved housekeeping

□ taking time and care

□ intervening when unsafe behaviour is observed

□ calculating risk

□ increased awareness of responsibility for the safety of oneself and others.

The team reviewed its own learning experiences by brainstorming and discussing what tended to work well and not so well in the past when they had to learn something. Their thinking fell into five broad categories:

□ team-based and group learning in preference to individually based learning

□ participative learning, enabling them to make contributions, being able to see the benefits from the outset, allowing self-teaching

□ activity-based learning in ways which permit looking in from outside, trial and error, doing and presenting projects, keeping things practical and making sense, and outdoor activities/learning

□ behaviour-focused learning, enabling personal improvement

□ high-impact learning with enough time to do it properly, use of multimedia, monetary gain or reward, knowledgeable/ enthusiastic people to present, being able to visualise end point, short busy sessions that bring benefits outside work.

In the light of all the exercises and discussions the team members created a draft framework of seven critical behaviours which they believed would result in a safer working environment for themselves and their colleagues. The draft behavioural safety framework created by the project team is shown below.

Coping with different pressures

□ reducing pressure on others
□ resisting pressure from others
□ staying calm.

Intervening

□ influencing others' behaviour positively by intervention, achieving co-operation, and recognising that priorities will be different
□ accepting intervention directly and positively
□ showing a good example
□ actively supporting the systems
□ seeking change and improvement
□ trying to get to the root cause of things.

Risk assessment

□ knowledge of plant/equipment and how it works
□ knowledge of what a job entails
□ ability to identify hazards and potential hazards
□ assessing, evaluating and taking action on risks, putting controls in place and recognising acceptable risks involved.

Involvement

□ confidently and actively contributing to giving information, bringing about change, planning, scheduling, modifications, projects and design.

Communication

- ☐ identifying where communication needs to improve
- ☐ taking steps to improve it.

Knowing, using and improving

- ☐ systems
- ☐ rules
- ☐ procedures.

'Being alive to safety' (going the extra mile)

- ☐ making things happen, rather than waiting for them to happen
- ☐ taking the initiative
- ☐ acting rather than 'acting'
- ☐ showing a good example
- ☐ actively supporting the systems
- ☐ seeking change and improvement
- ☐ trying to get to the root cause of things.

Finally, the team members planned the sessions at which they would present their proposals and invite feedback from all the people working in their own area. In keeping with the empowered team learning approach, it was decided that rather than 'tell' them the team's conclusions they would take their peers through some of the exercises that they had done themselves. This would allow their peers to draw their own conclusions before being presented with, and responding to, the project team's conclusions and recommendations. A day was set aside for the project team to design and prepare for the briefing sessions with their colleagues.

Step 9: Consulting

Having agreed the draft framework for behavioural safety on

site, the project team members planned group briefing sessions with all their peers. They wished to emphasise to their peers that the information was obtained from them, that they had the summarised findings presented to them for comment, and that the behavioural framework was essentially their framework. The briefing session was an additional opportunity for them to help and finalise the behavioural safety framework.

The purpose of the workshop was to plan in detail how to conduct the briefing sessions. The objectives were to

- discuss how to present the findings to the rest of the department
- plan in detail how to run the briefing sessions
- practise as necessary to ensure that the meetings would go well.

The facilitator guided the project team through the following questions on a worksheet, using the structured brainstorming technique described in Chapter 5.

- *What are we trying to achieve with the briefings?*
- *What could go wrong?*
- *What do you want to tell them?*
- *What do you want from them?*

To design the briefing sessions, the team members were asked by the facilitator to reflect on what they liked about the discussions they had experienced during the course of the project. In the light of this, the team decided on the features they should design into the briefing sessions and came up with:

- open dialogue – people should not feel inhibited from speaking their minds
- working in pairs – more creative; more supportive
- writing thoughts down – makes you concentrate; puts your brain in gear; clarifies your thoughts; makes it easier to say it
- someone in the role of facilitator to – pose the questions; hold the group together; direct the process and maintain

focus; promote open discussion; be neutral.

The team then clarified its own thinking on the project so that it was equipped to deal with the challenges and queries raised by their peers.

The team members ran the briefing sessions using a combination of presented information and facilitated discussion. They applied the facilitation skills they had developed over the course of the project through observing the facilitator and participating in practice sessions (and their own experience of running discussions). The actual plan they used for the briefing sessions is presented below.

1 Understanding of the project
   What is your understanding of this project?
   Write down words or phrases that come to mind when thinking about this project.
2 Understanding what we have done
   What would indicate to you that we have been really successful?
   What would prevent us from achieving it?
   What would constitute success?
3 Show our draft behaviour framework
   Now you understand the project, here is the outcome: this is our framework for a safe person.
   What do we mean by behaviour?
These are our examples of the behaviours we need to keep us safe.
4 Help us improve the behaviour framework
   Run the exercise to brainstorm additional positive and negative behaviour indicators.
5 Build understanding of effective learning
   What helps you learn well?
   What hinders your learning?
6 Ask them to suggest ways to learn
   What are your ideas on helping us learn these behaviours that you helped us to find?
   How confident do you feel that this is all going to work?
   What would increase your confidence?
   Finally, having heard all about the project and what we

have been doing, what would help make us more successful?

7 What else do you want us to do?

Step 10: Planning the implementation

In the light of the output and feedback from the briefing meetings, the project team members met to finalise the framework which would be used to bring about changes in the behaviour and attitudes of their peers and themselves. The objectives of the workshop were to

- ☐ review the outputs from the briefing sessions
- ☐ agree the positive and negative indicators for the safety-first behaviour framework
- ☐ agree the characteristics of effective learning modules for the safety-first behaviour framework
- ☐ specify in detail the design of learning modules
- ☐ agree the indicators for increased personal safety
- ☐ plan ahead.

The team reviewed the key messages and responses emerging from the briefing sessions and took the view that 'Alive to Safety' was a cohesive concept that tied the other six behaviours together. The behaviour framework was therefore named the 'Alive to Safety' Framework.

The facilitator then ran an exercise to deepen the team's understanding of the concept of behaviour. The word *honesty* was written on the flipchart and team members were asked how they would know that someone was honest. The responses were written up on the flipchart. In some cases the facilitator probed a response further by asking, 'How would we know that the person was ... *(the word or phrase under discussion)*,' and continued in this fashion until what was offered was a clear behaviour. A circle was drawn around it, and the facilitator invited more offerings from the group, putting a plus sign (+) against the circled items that were later identified as 'positive behaviour indicators' and a minus sign (−) against the items that were 'negative behaviour indicators'.

The group was then invited to compare the circled items

with those the facilitator had not circled. Through discussion, the criteria for a behavioural indicator were identified as:

□ observable
□ being based on a verb (and therefore comprising an activity)
□ relevant
□ unambiguous.

The next task was to add detail to the behavioural framework by adding illustrative positive and negative indicators to each of the six headings in the framework.

□ coping with different pressures
□ risk assessment
□ intervening
□ involvement
□ communication
□ knowing, using and improving (safety and working).

The team started with the first heading, 'Coping with different pressures' and, working in pairs, brainstormed possible indicators. These were discussed and modified to meet the behaviour criteria before being written on the flipchart. Once the team was clear about behavioural indicators, the collated lists of suggested indicators from the briefing sessions were circulated. The team set to work under the following instructions:

□ *Read through the negative and the positive indicators for 'assessing risk'.*
□ *Apply the standards for behaviour indicators and cross out any that do not qualify.*
□ *Then with your highlighter pen mark the ones you personally like.*
□ *Now choose the best positive and negative indicators and write them below. You can modify the words if you wish.*

This process was repeated for the remaining five behaviours using the lists of suggested behaviour indicators generated at the briefing sessions and reproduced in the workshop manual for the project team members. On the second day of the workshop the team analysed the desired features of the learning modules on behavioural safety which were also generated at the briefing sessions.

A practical exercise was used by the facilitator to deepen the team's understanding of how people learn. The exercise was adapted from Pearn and Mulrooney's *Tools for a Learning Organisation* (published by the Institute of Personnel and Development, 1995). The project team was divided into pairs and each pair was given a pack of 30 'How Do I Learn?' cards. The pairs were asked to sort them into three piles according to what was needed in order to learn the item on the card. Items included tasks such as 'riding a bike', 'typing', 'telephone numbers'. The pairs then discussed the categories with the rest of the team. Through discussion the team identified the key point that learning can be related to (i) *facts* which have to be memorised, (ii) *concepts* which have to be understood, and (iii) *activities* which are learned by doing.

The facilitator also introduced a discussion on the best ways to learn the items in each of the three piles and the role of errors in learning facts, concepts and activities. Some of the key points drawn out included the importance of trying to prevent errors from occurring when learning a physical skill, and the benefits of breaking the task down into parts and making sure each component part is thoroughly learned. Another key learning point was the importance of errors to improve understanding of concepts and issues.

Drawing on the improved understanding of learning processes gained from this exercise, and coupled with their past experience of learning, the team members brainstormed what they wanted to see and what they wished to avoid in the learning modules. Their ideas are shown below:

What we want to see in the 'Alive to Safety' learning modules:

☐ the responsibility for the design rests with us
☐ it is fun to do
☐ theory and practice are done together
☐ there is effective feedback

☐ there is co-operation with other functions/teams
☐ it is related to real life
☐ the benefits are obvious
☐ examples are practical
☐ the trainer/facilitator knows his/her stuff
☐ we are able to relate to our personal situation
☐ achievement is worth having.

What we want to avoid:

☐ its becoming lip-service (no buy-in)
☐ lecturing, being talked down to
☐ its not being integrated into our work
☐ dry, boring presentations
☐ learning something of no value
☐ instruction manuals, reams of paper
☐ a trainer with poor facilitation skills
☐ the theory without the practice
☐ being told to do it
☐ bad timing
☐ being rushed
☐ being afraid to be honest.

The team then worked through each behaviour heading of the framework in turn, discussing ideas on what to learn and how it would best be learned. Following further discussions, the project team decided real change would come about if they concentrated on only two categories of behaviour which they saw as most critical:

☐ understanding risk
☐ intervening and being intervened upon.

The project team members believed that if they could bring about significant shifts in these behaviours in themselves and their colleagues they would be able to make the site a measurably safer place. The full behavioural definitions of the two categories of safe behaviours are shown overleaf.

The overall goal: Alive to Safety

What we aspire to:

- ☐ We value other people's safety as well as our own.
- ☐ We take an active role on safety.
- ☐ We do not wait to be told.
- ☐ We are prepared to intervene and get involved.
- ☐ We take the safe way, even if it is the long way round.

What we want to leave behind:

- ☐ 'It's someone else's problem.'
- ☐ It has no interest.
- ☐ It accepts the way things are.
- ☐ It does not challenge.
- ☐ It makes fun of those who take safety seriously.
- ☐ It will probably cause hassle.
- ☐ It avoids getting involved.

Assessing risk

Positive behaviours

- ☐ makes discussion of risk part of task
- ☐ asks and thinks about worst-case scenario and consequences of actions
- ☐ looks for information and expert advice
- ☐ takes potential hazards into account when planning
- ☐ does not ignore hazards and takes action
- ☐ checks and re-checks

Negative behaviours

- ☐ makes assumptions and does not check
- ☐ continues a job when unsure of all the consequences
- ☐ does not admit when he/she does not know a job fully
- ☐ does not try to find safer way to do a job
- ☐ does not accept recognised hazards
- ☐ knowingly takes unacceptable risks
- ☐ does not wear appropriate safety gear for a task.

Intervening

Positive behaviours	Negative behaviours
□ offers and accepts advice and help	□ allows unsafe conduct to continue
□ seeks advice and help	□ mentions a problem to others, not the individual
□ intervenes if people act unsafely	□ argues rather than discusses
□ accepts others' intervening	□ tells others to mind their own business
□ communicates directly rather than going above people's heads	□ turns a blind eye to unsafe acts
□ stops a job if unsafe	□ will not accept interventions from others
	□ walks past a problem
	□ shows no interest in what others are doing

The one remaining objective to be addressed was to plan ahead. To prepare itself for this, the team first of all brainstormed the success indicators for the project as a whole. These included quantitative and qualitative measures:

Quantitative success indicators included:

□ a reduction in recorded accidents
□ an increase in Near Incidents/Accident (NIAs) *reports* (at least initially)
□ fewer Near Incidents/Accidents (NIAs) longer-term.

Qualitative success indicators included:

□ people are challenged for unsafe acts
□ greater involvement generally: more names on hazard logs, people at morning meetings, planning, etc
□ people in the day team give as much priority to safety.

Building on these success indicators, the team created its plans for the next phase:

☐ Create the 'Alive to Safety' mission as a poster campaign.

☐ Have a base-line audit done (possibly by the safety department).

☐ Initiate regular audits, two a week for the next four weeks, and start intervening at the end of the period, the audits to focus on unsafe practices (behaviour), and unsafe conditions to add to/subtract from the base-line audit.

☐ Create 'Alive to Safety' entries in the day log.

☐ Create an 'Alive to Safety' board and start graphing compliance levels.

☐ Each team member is to brief his/her own team as soon as possible with
   – a poster
   – the finalised 'Alive to Safety' behaviours
   – plans to start the regular audits
   – proposals for the learning modules.

☐ Do further design work on the specifications for the modules.

☐ Meet to finalise the specifications and agree the timetable, work to be done, and training needs of 'champions' to support the modules.

Step 11: Briefing

The project team members designed and ran workshops with everyone who worked in their area including all managers and specialists. The aim was to get the commitment of everyone to the 'Alive to Safety' framework. They incorporated some of the learning that they themselves had experienced into the workshops. The objectives of the workshops were to

☐ review the 'Alive to Safety' behaviours with the aim of getting everyone to sign up

☐ deepen the team's understanding and skills in assessing risk and intervening

☐ agree how the team would know and measure changes in behaviour that will lead to increased safety

☐ decide what else the team needed to do to ensure success.

The workshops were conducted by means of a combination of presenting information (eg the mission statement created by the project team, the 'Alive to Safety' framework, designed in consultation with people site-wide), and facilitated discussion.

The exercise on developing an understanding of risk assessment started with questions:

□ *We want you to think of two times when you felt at risk, one at work and the other not at work. Describe these to the other person in your pair under the following headings:*

   – Where were you?
   – When was it?
   – What happened (or did not happen)?

The factors that made them feel at risk were recorded on the flipchart and discussed by the participants. Guidelines were then created by the group for their own use. A similar approach was adopted on the whole issue of intervening when seeing someone else behaving in an unsafe way and accepting intervention from someone else.

Finally the participants' views of the project were captured. The peer group acknowledged the hard work put into the project by the team. The need for buy-in and commitment to the process by all was recognised. It was seen as an interesting and promising approach which had the potential to deliver. It provided a new and exciting perspective and heightened people's awareness of safety and the need to act safely.

Step 12: Review and monitoring

The project team continues to meet periodically to monitor progress against the agreed success indicators. The progress of the team has been significant, as conveyed by the following comments from Pat Sweeney, the human resources manager on site.

> The work of the members of the team has achieved a mind-set change among their colleagues and it has resulted in significant behavioural change and improved safety performance.
>
> The team members themselves changed from being scepti-

cal to actually facilitating learning situations for their colleagues. The facilitation process used was an important factor in achieving the change and commitment. The process facilitated a climate where individuals learned for themselves and from each other and the resulting commitment drove the change process.

Nelius Kennedy, the project co-ordinator had this to say:

> Organisations should never underestimate the talents of their people to affect change positively, particularly in areas in which they have a major stake. The process used is not for dabbling in: it needs commitment, perseverance, and faith in the people with whom it is entrusted. The bottom line is that the project team has succeeded in what it originally set out to do.

The 'Alive to Safety' behaviours are now accepted across the site. Discussions on behavioural safety have become part of everyday life at the plant. This is demonstrated by people's assessing risk when under pressure instead of rushing in. There is greater consistency across the various work teams. People are intervening more and challenging unsafe practices. People are also more open to intervention and receptive to feedback about their own behaviour and are more eager to implement recommendations that follow from safety audits. There is also less cynicism. Some safety procedures, such as tag-outs, have significantly improved, and benchmarked safety standards have also improved.

People on the site are taking more responsibility for their own safety, working together to generate ideas for combating hazardous situations. Risks are assessed more accurately and prompt action is taken to deal with potential hazards. There is a better team spirit overall, with everyone wearing the same 'safety hat'. People do not just complain any more – they now take action and follow things through.

The project team members grew in confidence over the course of the project and gained a number of critical skills, including interviewing, facilitation, data interpretation and planning skills. They also gained a sense of achievement from their involvement in the project, as reflected in the comment below (from team member Timmy Donegan):

This project was good because it came from the bottom up. It was attainable by everybody. Everyone's input mattered, no matter how great or how small. The project gave us the parameters to work within.

The next chapter takes a closer look at the skills needed to facilitate empowered team learning.

5 A STEP-BY-STEP GUIDE TO EMPOWERED TEAM LEARNING WORKSHOPS

In this chapter we describe the core facilitation process critical to the achievement of empowered team learning. We also describe the exact processes followed in the five key workshops.

The six core facilitation processes

The empowered team learning workshops are facilitated in a way that ensures that the team grows in its confidence to undertake the task in hand and learns as a team and as individual team members; develops a shared understanding of all the issues with which it is dealing; and retains ownership and responsibility for its thinking and actions.

There are six distinctive features of the empowered team learning facilitation process:

- brainstorming sessions
- the use of worksheets
- the Keys to Understanding
- reflection and review to consolidate learning
- learning to learn
- practical exercises for light relief.

Running the brainstorming sessions

The brainstorming sessions in empowered team learning workshops are a key feature that a team can feel reinforces the sense of its being completely in charge and not dependent on experts or other specialists. Many of the questions brainstormed by the team are based on the Keys to Understanding described later in this chapter. Typically, the facilitator divides the team into twos, presents the question to be brainstormed on a worksheet, and asks the pairs to write down anything that occurs to them. The members of each pair do not have to agree with one another, but working together frequently sparks more ideas and provides a degree of comfort for those who may initially feel uncomfortable about being asked to generate ideas in this way.

The facilitator usually focuses the team's attention on one or sometimes two related questions at a time. Often it is important to collate and review the output of one question on a flipchart before brainstorming the next question.

After about five to ten minutes, the facilitator asks each pair in turn for one of their ideas, and writes it up on the flipchart without evaluative comment, exactly as produced by the pair. Longer contributions are either broken down into specific points or deferred to allow others to contribute, once a specific point has been extracted from the pair. The facilitator proceeds around the room until all new points have been extracted and written up. A high degree of satisfaction is often felt by a team as the range and depth of its own thinking is displayed on the flipchart. Usually two or three questions are brainstormed before the combined output is used for some purpose, which might include:

☐ applying agreed criteria to make a choice
☐ making decisions
☐ creating a plan
☐ agreeing performance standards
☐ agreeing a mission statement
☐ prioritising
☐ defining options
☐ analysing a problem
☐ finding solutions.

Brainstorming is the core process by which the team develops its own shared understanding and creates various outputs. There is a growing realisation within the team that no one member could produce the same output, and that the quality of its collective thinking is at least as good and often superior to that of so-called experts or their managers. This is an enormous confidence-boost to the team.

Even at later stages in empowered team learning the team should not let go of brainstorming as the prime source of collective thinking and decision-making. It is important that team leaders do not attempt to direct the team in its thinking. Continued commitment to brainstorming will ensure that the team thinks and makes decisions collectively on all important issues.

The use of worksheets

Worksheets are critical to empowered team learning. Writing down responses to brainstormed questions imposes a discipline on the facilitator and the team itself. The use of worksheets may seem strange and somewhat artificial at first, but once the team has experienced the benefits, the use of worksheets quickly becomes popular amongst its members because

- it allows them to develop their thoughts before having to speak
- it enhances the feeling that all the members of the team are equals
- shy individuals learn to speak up and share their ideas
- dominant individuals learn to give others space.

It is not always necessary to use prepared worksheets, but it is a good idea in the initial workshops to develop the habit of using them. At later stages it might be sufficient to write the questions to be brainstormed on a flipchart and ask the team members to write down their thoughts on a piece of paper. As the team members grow in confidence it may not always be necessary to maintain the discipline of using prepared questions for brainstorming, working in pairs, and writing down thoughts before writing them all on a flipchart. In practice, however, many teams prefer to maintain these disciplined procedures even after the point when openness, trust, and mutual respect amongst their members have been achieved.

The Keys to Understanding

The Keys to Understanding is a technique for formulating and sequencing the brainstorming questions which are designed to deepen a group's shared understanding of an issue before making use of the understanding in some way. The approach is described in Pearn *et al* (1995), and practical exercises to develop the skills of writing and using the Keys to Understanding can be found in Pearn and Mulrooney's *Tools for a Learning Organisation* (IPD, 1995).

There are five main Keys to Understanding questions:

The purposes – What are all the possible purposes that can be served by ...?

This question has been applied during empowered team learning workshops to develop a better understanding of performance management, create a plan, write a clear mission statement, achieve behavioural safety, and run an information-gathering exercise. It is nearly always the first question brainstormed during a workshop or a key phase within a workshop. The purpose questions work best if they take the group back to fundamentals. Instead of brainstorming how to improve a safety procedure, for example, it is helpful for the group to brainstorm why it has procedures at all with the question 'What are all the possible purposes of procedures?'

One or two other Keys to Understanding questions should then be brainstormed before the team attempts to apply its new shared understanding to address an issue.

The problems – What would be the consequences if...? or What problems could arise if...?

The problems question serves to widen the team's thinking and to reinforce its commitment to addressing an issue seriously. The output obtained from brainstorming this question often broadens the team's perspective.

The viewpoints – How would ... be seen from the viewpoint of ...?

Viewpoint questions also serve to widen the team's thinking on an issue. For example:

☐ What are the benefits of increased behavioural safety to
  – us?
  – our families?
  – the local community?

  – management?
  – the company?
  – others?

The contrasts – In what ways is ... similar to/different from ...? or How would you like ... to be similar to/different from ...?

  ☐ Thinking back over when you had to learn things in the past, what would you like to be the same, and what would you like to be different?

Contrast and comparison questions serve to widen the team's thinking but also to establish common ground. The contrast question has been used to good effect in several empowered team learning projects when teams designed learning interventions. The question was also powerful in helping to understand all the actual and potential differences and similarities between directly employed and contract drivers.

The evaluation – How might we tell if we have ... succeeded, understood, etc?

  Evaluation or checking questions are powerful both in broadening the team's thinking and also in helping it to focus on critical aspects of the project at the outset of the project rather than at later stages when choices and options may be more restricted. By creating an evaluation framework at the outset the team not only deepens its understanding of the issue(s) being addressed but also pre-empts problems that could arise at later stages.

  One of the features of empowered team learning workshops is that issues are addressed on an ongoing basis. For example, the question 'How might we tell if we have succeeded?' can be brainstormed at the outset of a project but also during its successive stages.

Reflection and review sessions to consolidate learning

  At the end of each workshop, and at critical points along the way, the facilitator runs reflection and review sessions. The sessions are important in enabling individual members of the team to articulate what is important for them personally and to hear what others are thinking. It is essential not to leave the reflection and review session until the end of the workshop because corrective action may be too late by this time and individual members may have learned not to say what they really think. A three-day workshop might have three or four formal reflection and review sessions focusing on the preceding sessions, and one reflection and review session for the workshop as a whole.

Encouraging team members to reflect in silence and write down their thoughts enriches the reflection and review session. Following a systematic procedure to allow each member to talk in turn reinforces the feeling of openness and equality between team members.

Reflection and review sessions are usually based on the following questions:

□ *What, for you personally, were the key learning points from today's sessions?*
□ *What implications do you see for yourself?*
□ *What implications do you see for the team?*

The reflection and review session at the end of the workshop poses the question:

□ *What do you think we as a team have achieved during this workshop?*

The ABCD structure can be useful for more formal reflection and review sessions:

1 Achievements
2 Benefits
3 Concerns
4 Do next.

Learning to learn

The facilitator incorporates sessions that are specifically designed to give the team an insight into the learning process and at the same time to build learning-to-learn skills. This is most critical if the team initially feels nervous and somewhat overawed by the task it has undertaken.

Asking the team to brainstorm the things that hinder and help learning, followed by a discussion on how to minimise learning 'blockers' and maximise 'enablers', gives the team a feeling of being in control of its own learning. This process is especially powerful if the team is in a position to influence the way it brings about learning.

Another exercise that has proved helpful is Learning to Question in Pearn and Mulrooney's *Tools for a Learning Organisation* (IPD 1995). The team learns to perform a reasonably complex task solely by asking the facilitator questions. These questions are recorded as they are being asked. The facilitator answers only the questions that are asked and does not give any other help. Eventually all the members of the team learn to perform the task. The facilitator then asks the team members to identify from the recorded questions which ones were most helpful to them at the time they were asked. The nature of the most helpful questions is then reviewed by the team. They tend to be short, open, and frequently fall into the five Keys to Understanding.

Powerful learning points that emerge from this exercise include the fact that by *not* asking questions team members can inhibit their own learning. Some questions give more control to the learner. Questioning is a skill which improves with practice, and some questions work better if asked earlier rather than later.

This questioning exercise boosts the confidence of team members to learn, as they see the Keys to Understanding playing a critical role in helping them develop their thinking and progressively achieve successful outcomes.

Practical exercises for light relief

The empowered team learning workshops can be quite demanding on the team members. There are virtually no lectures, presentations, or formal inputs during the workshop in which individual team members can lean back and take it easy, confident in the knowledge that they will not have to contribute. Because most of the empowered team learning workshop sessions involve paired working, small group, and plenary brainstorming and decision-making, individual team members can find the process mentally demanding.

Consequently, it is important to build into the workshop design frequent breaks and sessions that enable the participants to do something different.

Physical team learning exercises provide the necessary contrast, are usually enjoyable, and provide an opportunity to gain further insight into how individual members operate as a team. Experience has shown that the energy, creativity and well-being of the team diminishes rapidly in the absence of one or more physical team learning exercises on each day of a workshop. Competitive team exercises which involve learning to tie nautical knots or juggling balls have proved flexible and popular.

Facilitating an Empowered Team Learning Workshop

There are five empowered team learning workshops (see Figure 6). The core facilitation processes involved in each workshop are described below.

Facilitating Workshop A – Exploring the issues

The duration of the exploratory workshop is typically one or two days. The aim is to begin the process of deepening the team's shared understanding of, and commitment to, the project. The team members begin to realise that they have control of the project, are being trusted with the task, and that it is up to them to make it work.

The formal objectives usually take this form:

1 Develop a shared understanding of the project aims.
2 Clarify the role of the project team.
3 Define objectives.
4 Map out the main steps of the project.
5 Identify performance and success indicators.
6 Agree an action plan and timetable.

The meeting begins with brief introductions. The facilitator explains that his or her role is to facilitate and support the team members in the achievement of their project aims, but not to lead them. The facilitator reviews the objectives of the meeting and states that much of the thinking and

Figure 6
KEY WORKSHOPS IN EMPOWERED TEAM LEARNING

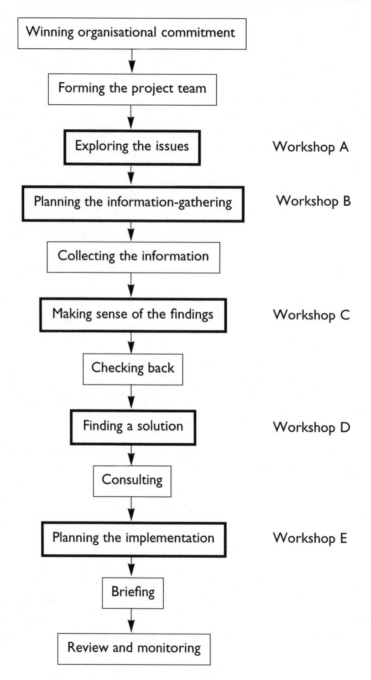

decision-making required will be done by structured brain-storming.

In most cases the members of the team would have received some form of briefing when they were invited to join the project. The facilitator suggests that team members pool their thoughts and knowledge about the project using the brainstorming process described earlier.

The facilitator refers them to the questions on the work-sheet and asks them, working in pairs, to spend about five to ten minutes writing down anything that comes to mind.

☐ *Based on what you already know about the project, what words or phrases come to mind?*

☐ *How would you like this project to be different from other projects in which you have been involved? In what ways would you like it to be similar?*

Each pair is then asked for one of the words or expressions they have written down in response to Question 1. It is written up on a flipchart by the facilitator without comment or evaluation, who proceeds around the room until all new words and expressions have been written on the flipchart.

The facilitator now invites the team to comment on what has been said, highlighting the words or phrases which accurately convey what the project is about. The team is then asked to brainstorm the ingredients of a good mission statement. The ideas are written on the flipchart and the criteria for a good mission statement are agreed. The team is then split into groups of three or four and each group is asked to draft a possible mission statement in about 30 minutes. Each group then presents its draft (mission statement) on a flipchart to the others, and the whole team agrees which components of the drafts it would like to see in a final mission statement. The team then brainstorms and agrees the values that it wishes to guide its work.

The next phase of the meeting is to plan the overall project. In order to do this the facilitator poses more questions, again on a worksheet, for the team members to brainstorm in pairs.

☐ *What are the possible benefits of developing a project plan?*

☐ *How might we tell if we are being successful?*
☐ *What must we take into account to ensure we are successful?*

About 20 to 30 minutes is allowed for generating ideas and the process outlined previously is used to collate all the responses on a flipchart. The issues raised are discussed by the group for about 20 minutes before another brainstorming question is posed by the facilitator (again on a worksheet).

☐ *In carrying out this project what could go wrong?*

The facilitator assists the team in putting together an action plan in the light of all the items that have been raised.
A key phase of empowered team learning is some form of information-gathering from peers, colleagues and other sources judged by the team to be relevant.
The facilitator therefore asks the team now to think about how to prepare for the task of gathering this information. The team brainstorms the main issues on which it would like more information, and in the light of the combined output a tentative framework is agreed.

Facilitating Workshop B – Planning the information-gathering

The duration of the workshop is typically two or three days. The team reviews the output from the previous workshop and decides on the information needed, and the people from whom it should get this information. It then decides on the actual questions it wants to ask, and practises the skills of asking questions and recording the answers given to them. It also decides on the methods to be used (eg individual interviews, group discussions) and plans the logistics of the data-gathering process. The team agrees its own performance indicators for the information-gathering exercise.
Objectives for the workshop usually take the form:

1 Review the outputs of the previous meeting and finalise the objectives of the information-gathering process.
2 Write the questions to be asked during the audit.
3 Plan the data-gathering process in detail.
4 Practise asking questions and recording the answers.

5   Think ahead to later phases in the project.

6   Agree the performance measures for the project.

The facilitator firstly invites the group to review the typed-up outputs (the flipcharts) from the previous meeting and to agree any changes. The team is then asked in pairs to brainstorm the question:

☐ *What do you think could go wrong during the information-gathering discussions?*

Once the ideas/items generated have been collated on the flipchart, the project team suggests ways of dealing with the problems identified. Typical problems raised include:

☐ mistrust
☐ difficulties in recording the information
☐ insincerity
☐ the interviewer may not have knowledge of or interest in the survey
☐ no commitment from management
☐ holidays
☐ time
☐ interruptions
☐ noise/distractions
☐ the interviewer takes over
☐ the interviewee does not communicate
☐ the wording of the questions – intonation
☐ interviewers contradict/conflict with each other
☐ silly answers
☐ refusal to answer
☐ not keeping the appointment.

The facilitator avoids presenting theory and instead uses the output of brainstorming sessions to develop guidelines and to make decisions to improve the quality and reliability of the information obtained. The team comes up with its own ideas on how to overcome the various problems that it foresees.

The facilitator asks the team to brainstorm all the things

that should go into the introduction and closing of an interview. A checklist for introducing and closing an interview is
then agreed. The facilitator asks the team, in pairs, to draft
the actual questions they would like to ask under the agreed
category headings. The proposed wording for the questions is
then modified in plenary discussion using criteria brainstormed by the team.

The facilitator then asks the team to split into threes and
to take it in turns for two of them to interview the third
person on one of the questions, using the agreed checklist for
opening and closing the interview. The facilitator uses the
Learning Spiral approach described in Chapter 3.

Afterwards, the threes come together and the facilitator
asks what they have learned from the experience. The checklists and agreed guidelines are then modified in the light of
this experience. The facilitator asks the threes to practise on
another question before the learning points are reviewed and
the guidelines finalised. The team then agrees on the pairs
who will conduct the interviews and establishes the categories and names of the people they will interview during
the chosen period following the workshop. If focus groups are
to be used, the facilitator provides opportunities to practise,
reflect on the experience and revise both the process and the
evolving guidelines in the light of experience.

The project team then agrees a date on which to hold a
meeting to review progress. This is usually set to allow some
of the data-gathering to be done but not so much that any
changes in process or the questions after the review would
seriously upset the whole exercise.

Facilitating the interim review meeting
The duration of the interim review meeting is typically a half
to a whole day. It is held to check on progress, exchange
experiences, make changes to the information-gathering
process in the light of experience, and improve the guidance
material created at the planning workshop.

The objectives typically take the form:

1 Review progress of the project as a whole.
2 Discuss any feedback and review how the interviews and
   information-gathering is going.

3 Review the nature of the information being obtained and practical issues around the wording of questions, timing, structure and skills needs.
4 Agree changes.
5 Plan the remaining phases of the information-gathering.
6 Review what happens next.

The facilitator opens the meeting by asking each person in turn to say how he or she feels the project is going. Any problems or concerns are recorded, discussed, and dealt with in a supportive manner. The facilitator then poses two questions:

☐ *What has gone well in the information-gathering so far?*
☐ *What did not work so well?*

All the team members are asked to write down their views before they are recorded on the flipchart and opened up to general discussion. If necessary, the team discusses and changes the wording of some of the questions or the introduction. They also discuss and agree other ways to improve the information-gathering process and the quality of the information being obtained.

The gathered data is collated and presented in a manageable form but is not summarised or interpreted before the team meets.

Facilitating Workshop C – Making sense of the findings

The duration of this workshop is usually two or three days. At the start of the workshop, the team is encouraged to stand back from the detail of the information-gathering and to brainstorm the main issues. The team then learns the skills of summarising and coding information as it systematically works through the data-gathering.

Objectives typically take the form

1 Review how well the information-gathering has gone.
2 Identify the main themes that have emerged.
3 Learn how to summarise and code the information collected.
4 Plan how to summarise the findings back to the people involved in the information-gathering.

The facilitator starts by clarifying the objectives of the workshop and stresses that a picture of the findings will unfold over two (or three) days and that it will be hard work. However, there will be lots of short breaks, and they should feel free to ask for them, or to walk about, etc.

The facilitator asks each member of the team to say how he or she feels about the information-gathering, and the high and low spots of the process. The facilitator then reminds them that they must have many impressions of the information gained from the data-gathering and invites the team members to close the files containing the data and process, sit back and reflect on the key issues or trends.

The facilitator asks the team members, working in pairs, to brainstorm the key issues or ideas that emerged from the interviews or discussions which they conducted. The items emerging are collated on a flipchart and are reviewed and classified into the framework that makes most sense to the team. The framework provides the basis for the subsequent analysis of the data and is amended and modified as the analysis proceeds.

The facilitator asks the team, working in pairs, to read completely through the first section of typed-up interviews and mark with a highlighter pen all the items that they think confirm their initial framework in one colour, and all the items that enlarge or extend their initial view with another. The facilitator then leads a group discussion to draw out the criteria for establishing the relevance of the findings.

Starting with one pair, the facilitator asks them to refer to all the items they have identified as relevant from the answers to Question 1 of the survey, and asks whether the other pairs agree. If not, the facilitator draws the differences out in discussion. The idea is to get the group to develop a common understanding of the task they are undertaking. Starting with a different pair each time the facilitator follows this process to proceed through all the questions.

The underlying objective is to familiarise the team with the range and variety of information available, and to get the team members used to classifying and coding it before they discuss emerging conclusions. It also helps to identify which questions in the interview plan are going to be the most fruitful in addressing a particular area of concern.

When all the items have been marked and discussed, the facilitator leads a discussion to review and revise the framework which resulted from the initial brainstorming of key issues. The facilitator then asks the group to create rules to guide their own analysis (in effect, to create the team's own quality assurance rules).

The team members then create a plan for tackling the rest of the data, bearing in mind the number and sources of the interviews, and other pieces of relevant information they have available to them.

The facilitator runs a review and reflection session to assess how the team feels about the information it is interpreting and to help clarify the thinking of individual members.

The facilitator helps the team gradually take on ever larger chunks of the data by firstly establishing the relevance of the information and then coding it as relevant to, or extending, the initial framework. This cannot really be specified in advance and the facilitator works within the capabilities of the group.

Few people are accustomed to the disciplined and demanding nature of systematic data-analysis. It is important for the facilitator to recognise this and to review periodically how the team feels about the exercise, and encourage the team to stick close to the data. Also, because of the concentration involved in the process the facilitator should provide plenty of breaks as well as physical team learning exercises to provide refreshment and contrast.

All the remaining interviews are then analysed with a view to agreeing tentative conclusions. Once the facilitator is confident that the team is working reasonably well and consistently, it can be divided into smaller working groups, each one focusing on the same section of data but with different interviews.

The facilitator needs to allow several hours to review and agree the draft findings and to plan the next phase of the project, which is to run sessions with everyone the team interviewed and summarise the findings. At this stage the team has not attempted to draw conclusions or spell out implications that go beyond the data. It has summarised and made sense of the data, and needs to check back with those from whom the data was gathered that this summary accurately reflects what was said to the team during the information-gathering process.

At the checking-back sessions the team validates its findings before attempting to draw any conclusions. In this way it keeps close to the constituency of stakeholders from whom the information was obtained. The data should be seen as belonging to the constituency rather than to the team – a perception that is critical to the success of empowered team learning.

The team plans the checking-back sessions using the following questions:

- *Who should be involved?*
- *In what way?*
- *By when?*
- *What could go wrong in the sessions, and how prevented?*

The facilitator guides the team through a discussion to design the session by focusing on

- the reasons for the project
- the scope of the information-gathering exercise
- the questions posed
- the people interviewed
- the main findings that can be gathered
- the feedback from them by asking:
  - *What are your reactions to this summary?*
  - *Does it look accurate and realistic to you?*
  - *What advice or ideas do you have to offer us?*

Facilitating Workshop D – Finding a solution

The duration of this workshop is typically two or three days, depending on the complexity of the desired outcome. In some cases more than one design workshop may be necessary. The team meets to distil all the information, including the feedback obtained from the checking-back sessions, and agree a detailed specification for the outcome of the project.

Typically the objectives take the form:

1 Review feedback from the checking-back sessions.

2 Agree the lessons learned and their implications.

3 Agree a detailed specification for the proposed solution.

4 Discuss and agree the practical implications.

The facilitator asks each individual to write down on a sheet of paper the main points he or she saw coming out of the checking-back sessions before asking each person in turn for one of the points he or she has written down. The facilitator then helps the team to agree on the main issues arising from the sessions.

The facilitator asks the team (in pairs), using a worksheet, to brainstorm the possible factors in their environment that could cause or contribute to the issue under discussion. The facilitator writes up on a flipchart all the ideas produced by the group, and then clusters them into between six and 10 broad categories.

The aim of the exercise is to develop a shared understanding within the team of the complexity and interdependency of a wide range of relevant factors. This can be a difficult exercise for the team and requires skilful facilitation. The group is likely to experience frustration – but it is important to do this exercise.

The facilitator builds up on a flipchart an ever more complex diagram of the interrelationships between the identified factors before asking the team, in small groups of three or four, to come up with suggestions on how the key factors might be influenced or changed.

This exercise works best if the facilitator first talks the team through a worked illustration using a simplified diagram. This enables the facilitator to build up a feeling in the team for the complexity of the situation and draw out the key roles played by different kinds of factors. At this stage the facilitator is not trying to achieve consensus within the group, but is helping the team enrich its collective thinking. An example of the interplay of factors contributing to sustained risk of accidents was shown in Chapter 4.

The next step is to brainstorm those things that are already helping or can help to secure desired change (enablers) and the factors that could be obstructing or interfering with it (blockers). The facilitator uses a worksheet with the following questions:

- *What needs to change?*
- *When deciding what to focus on, what things should we take into account?*
- *What do we consider are the main priorities?*

Following plenary discussion two further questions are introduced on a worksheet to identify blockers and enablers:

- *If we want these things to change, what are the enablers and what are the potential blockers?*

On the following day the team develops ideas on what action can be taken. The facilitator presents a typed-up list of what people said needed to be changed at the checking-back sessions. Working in pairs, the team members use highlighter pens to mark all the suggestions that meet the previously brainstormed and agreed criteria. These are then collated on a flipchart and grouped into clusters. The clusters are prioritised again according to agreed criteria, and the team gradually agrees the actions it wishes to recommend at subsequent briefing sessions.

The team then plans the briefing sessions that are to be run with all the people who will be affected by its recommendations. The facilitator encourages the team members to avoid a tell-and-sell session. Instead, the people attending the briefings should be taken through some of the exercises or thinking processes that the team itself has undertaken. This allows the participants to develop their own individual thinking, before being presented with, and then responding to, the team's conclusions and recommendations.

The facilitator helps the team plan the briefing sessions. The participants at the briefing should be reminded that the information was obtained from them, that they had the findings presented to them for comment, and that the output is therefore essentially theirs. The facilitator guides the team through the following questions, adopting the usual process for structured brainstorming:

- *What are we trying to achieve?*
- *What could go wrong?*
- *What are you going to tell them?*
- *What do you want from them?*

In this way the team clarifies its own thinking so that it is better equipped to face the challenges and queries from its peers.

The facilitator introduces a few more questions designed to reveal to the team some of the underlying processes that enabled its own discussions to be productive and enjoyable:

☐ *What have you liked about the way our discussions as a team have been conducted?*

☐ *How can we incorporate this into our consultation sessions?*

The plan for the sessions is created by the team.

Facilitating Workshop E – Planning the implementation

Depending on the complexity of the task, the duration of this workshop is usually two or three days. In the light of the outputs and feedback collected from the consultation, the team meets to finalise the implementation plan that will bring about the changes agreed. The team also discusses and plans how to progressively monitor and evaluate the impact of any changes that are made.

The objectives typically take the form:

1 Review the outputs and feedback collected from the brief ing sessions.
2 Specify in detail the implementation plan.
3 Agree the success indicators for the project as a whole.
4 Plan how to measure impact and monitor progress.

The facilitator begins by posing the questions:

☐ *What were the key messages and responses coming from the consultation sessions?*

☐ *What changes do we need to make in the light of feedback from the sessions?*

The output is logged on a flipchart and the team agrees the actions to be taken. The facilitator then reviews all the ideas for monitoring and evaluating the success of the project by asking:

□ *What do you think are the most important success indicators?*

The facilitator then assesses the team's level of confidence and morale in response to the consultation with the following question:

□ *How confident do you feel that the project is going to be successful?*

After the group's views have been collated on a flipchart, the team finalises its implementation plan in the light of all the feedback from the consultation sessions.

In this chapter we described the core facilitation processes involved in empowered team learning, and the actual processes followed in the five key empowered team learning workshops. In the next chapter we present four detailed case-studies which illustrate different aspects of empowered team learning in practice.

6   EMPOWERED TEAM
LEARNING CASE-STUDIES

Introduction

In this chapter we describe four applications of empowered team learning:

☐ matching the skills of the unemployed to local employers' needs

☐ designing and implementing a performance management system

☐ overcoming the isolation felt by owner-managers of small businesses

☐ changing 'the way we do things round here'.

In each of them, sufficient detail of the processes involved in facilitating the key workshops is given to enable a skilled facilitator to replicate them.

The first case-study tells how a group of unemployed people discover through empowered team learning that they can design and carry out a survey which impresses local employers. The team of unemployed people develop self-confidence and overcome their fears and the learned insecurities about their worth as potential employees. This transformation comes about principally as a result of the team's survey findings which it presents to local employers; it is also encouraged by the gradual process of developing a shared understanding of issues, shared decision-making, and learning collectively with no dependence on experts or officials.

The most satisfying aspect of this story for us is that the qualities and abilities the team members discovered or developed as a result of empowered team learning were clearly recognised by local employers.

The second case-study focuses on an all too common problem in industry – the failure of one part of an organisation to talk to and understand another. Put another way, it looks at the problems which exist when different parts or functions of an organisation are not aligned but instead work to their own agendas, pulling apart rather than together. Classic symptoms of this are 'them and us' thinking, the not-invented-here syndrome, a general lack of co-ordination and co-operation, resulting in inefficiencies caused by a lack of synergy.

The case describes the use of empowered team learning to bring together line managers from different companies within a group which had previously lived with a high degree of independent thinking and operating despite attempts to apply consistent policies from the corporate centre.

Empowered team learning was used because it brought together a representative group of line managers from the different companies within the group and gave them collective responsibility for an important task. The team was asked to design and implement a performance management system that they knew would work. The absence of a formal leader within the group and the development of shared understanding and decision-making enabled the group to develop a specification for the performance management system which was likely to have credibility with all their colleagues in the different companies within the group.

The team designed a consultation process with a representative cross-section of managers within the group from the managing director downwards. Because of the empowered way in which they had developed their own thinking, the team was keen to ensure that the consultation process involved genuine two-way dialogue. This enabled them to obtain genuinely helpful feedback, which improved the specification for the performance management system that they had created while at the same time achieving employee acceptance and buy-in.

The third case-study describes empowered team learning applied to a group of owner-managers of small businesses. Empowered team learning enabled the owner-managers to form themselves into a network, create their own mission statement and eventually become self-managing without any external support. By brainstorming key issues, developing a shared understanding, and systematically trying to understand each other's companies, the members of the network learned to overcome the isolation and pressures they experienced as managers of small businesses.

They learned to share information and expertise, develop themselves as managers, and address the human resource issues they faced in their businesses. They achieved results by working together and learning from each other in a way that would not have been possible had they not formed the network. Above all, they learned to take charge of their personal and collective learning.

The final application of empowered team learning addresses another common problem in companies facing change. How do you get everyone to accept the need for change in a way that results in lasting changes in the organisation? The experience of many organisations is that change initiatives are seen as the flavour of the month and as a result have rapidly diminishing impetus with the passage of time. Often the words and the actions of senior managers are not congruent. This sends out confusing signals, to employees, causing or confirming widespread scepticism in the organisation.

Empowered team learning was used because it provided everyone in the organisation with an opportunity to have a say in how things should change. The survey was designed and carried out by a representative team of employees who identified the issues and formulated the questions for themselves. Because the team carried out the data-gathering and the summarising and interpretation of the information collected in such a rigorous way, they were able to keep close to their constituency and therefore assess the true feelings of the majority of employees.

The absence of intermediaries such as specialists, experts or people in a leadership role within the team also helped to convey the fact that the survey was an open and honest assessment of what employees had to say. The effect was to overcome the normal resistance of employees to change and the cynicism they feel about management-led top-down change initiatives. Some of the strongest feelings to be expressed were loyalty to the company, a desire to be part of a success story, and a desire to contribute to a company making the fullest use of the talents of its human resources.

Case-study 1

MATCHING THE SKILLS OF THE UNEMPLOYED TO LOCAL EMPLOYERS' NEEDS

The Local Employment Services (LES) in Limerick was established in 1995 and represents a model of excellence for other employment services in Ireland. The overall aim of the LES is to provide an independent, integrated, and personalised service which will meet the needs of its target groups:

☐ the long-term unemployed

☐ those unemployed for six to 12 months

☐ dependent spouses

☐ lone parents

☐ people with disabilities.

By providing information, guidance, mediation and placement, the LES empowers these target groups to find suitable employment. Empowered team learning is consistent with the underlying philosophy of the LES because it equips people with the skills to enable them to gain employment for themselves. The LES therefore saw the potential benefits of using this approach as a skills development and confidence-building process for the team members. Further possible benefits included the likely credibility of the survey findings, given that a representative team from the LES target groups would itself be carrying out the study, and given the cost-effectiveness of the approach if data-gathering was spread among the team members, and their skills drawn on by the LES during future projects.

The team was made up of eight people from target groups from different geographical regions within the LES catchment area, and two employees from the LES. The team had no prior experience of carrying out surveys and for many of the members it was the first time they had ever worked as part of a team.

The terms of reference were:

1 to identify and draw together existing research conducted on
    a) the employment skills of the Local Employment Service target
        groups

b)   the potential employment opportunities in the Limerick region

2   to survey the target population to establish a comprehensive picture of its skills and interests in relation to these employment opportunities

3   to draw together a comprehensive picture of other employment opportunities in the region

4   to make recommendations on how the Local Employment Service could address the training needs of the target group to enable it to successfully compete for the employment opportunities identified.

An initial two-day workshop was held to prepare the team for the project. The key objectives of this workshop were:

1   Develop the team's understanding of the purpose of the project.

2   Agree how best to carry out the project.

3   Jointly plan the whole project.

4   Develop and practise data-gathering skills.

5   Prepare for the next stages.

In order to develop their understanding of the purpose of the project, the team members initially considered what could be achieved from the consultation. The following questions were used by the facilitator to brainstorm the team's ideas:

☐   *What are the possible benefits or purposes of consulting with (i) the long-term unemployed and (ii) employers (assuming it is successful)?*

☐   *What could go wrong in a consultation exercise of this kind?*

Instead of lecturing the team on the best methods of gathering data, a number of open questions were used by the facilitator to encourage team members to consider and decide on the best course of action for the data-gathering stage.

☐   *What information do you think we might need?*

☐   *How and where might we obtain this information?*

☐   *What do you think are the pros and cons of different information gathering methods?*

Having brainstormed these questions and discussed them in plenary session, the team decided on two main techniques to gather the data: *a)* structured interviews and *b)* focus group discussions.

Structured interviews were to be used to gather information from target group members and employers. The importance of asking pertinent and properly phrased questions, of probing and of recording the information required was discussed. The team developed its own questions which members piloted on each other and refined accordingly. An introduction and further guidelines for interviewing were developed by the team in the light of the experience gained through these practice sessions.

Feedback obtained from the team after the exploratory workshop conveyed the level of enthusiasm felt for the approach, and reflected the team's growing confidence in its ability to self-manage the task at hand.

The team identified key respondents for its survey, and discussed the need for a representative sample. The following criteria were applied in devising a sampling frame for the target groups:

☐ gender
☐ age
☐ type of benefit received
☐ length of unemployment
☐ level of education.

This sampling frame ensured that a good mix of people was sampled and that the information gathered was therefore representative of the Limerick region. One hundred and thirty-eight people were surveyed during the study.

Although the team members had no difficulty in interviewing their peers, they were initially apprehensive about interviewing employers. The thought of the tables being turned – interviewing employers rather than being interviewed by them – was daunting to some. However, the team members discussed their fears and came to the conclusion that they should not be afraid of the task at hand, given that they had the necessary skills to carry out the interviews effectively. Some team members emphasised that preparation was the key to success, and that the team members had certainly done their preparation. They had faith in the tools they had created, which were standard introductions, interview schedules and guidelines.

The project team interviewed 33 employers from a range of sectors, including retail, manufacturing, services and hotel and catering. The key objective of these interviews was to uncover the employment opportunities that existed in the area and to find out how employers perceived people who were long-term unemployed.

Pilot interviews were held, followed by a review. This resulted in changes being made to the team's briefing documents in the light of its experiences, and the creation of checklists for introducing the interviews to ensure consistency across the team. The team also decided at this review meeting that it was necessary to allocate time to summarising notes immediately an interview had been conducted.

A quality check was conducted by the team during the data-collection stage. This interim review provided a forum to discuss the sampling to date and to plan further data collection from target groups who were not adequately represented. The review also helped to ensure consistency across the team, in terms of detail, objectivity, and relevance of the information gathered.

During the review, team members discussed their experiences of the interview process and advice was shared on how to overcome any difficulties encountered. The core team review assisted in the development of the team's research skills.

The key learning points to emerge from the review were the importance of writing notes immediately after an interview, the need for a review after an initial sample of interviews so that the briefing documents might be refined in the light of experience, and the need to take stock of the sample group and ensure that a representative sample is being targeted.

At the workshop, to make sense of findings, a data-analysis process was used to cluster the information collected under meaningful headings. Because of the quantity of the data this was a lengthy task. An initial process involved brainstorming the key themes, and subsequent analysis used these themes as a framework for categorising the information.

During this workshop the target group representatives learned the key skills of data analysis.

The team members liked the structure of this workshop, which enabled them to analyse and make sense of a wide range of information with relatively little difficulty. People were rotated to different tasks over the course of the two days and also had the opportunity to work in different subgroups of the team.

During a final review meeting, the information that had been analysed in the previous workshop was reviewed in the context of the project's four terms of reference. The team was divided into four groups to consider the information relevant to each one of the terms. Comments from the qualitative analysis were categorised to support the quantitative information. The team read through the comments elicited during the course of the data-collection process and linked them in with the key quantitative findings. These comments provided important insights into respondents' perceptions of people who were long-term unemployed.

In addition, the team members agreed the content and structure of their final report. Working in small teams they began to draft the contents of the report. This was then typed up by a member of the team.

The project team's report was entitled *Employment skills of target groups and potential employment opportunities* and launched at an Open Day for local employers. The team formally presented the report to an audience of over 150 people. Each member took responsibility for presenting a section of the report, and the team designed its own visual aids.

For most of the team members this was an anxious experience because they had no prior experience of formal presentations. The reasoning behind the presentation, however, was that it was the team members' project, they had done the work, and they were in the best position to present the findings to others. They had developed a great sense of ownership for the report.

One of the key outputs from the project was a skills register of people who are long-term unemployed in the Limerick region. Many of the respondent group were discovered to have clerical skills (secretarial, typing and book-keeping) and service skills (childcare, cleaning and security). The majority of the people surveyed had gained these skills prior to becoming unemployed, although one-third of them had participated in further training after becoming unemployed. Most of them recognised the importance of training, but there was frustration expressed by some as a result of not securing a job following one or more training courses. The value of some courses for gaining employment was questioned – eg aromatherapy and 'interior design for an Italian villa'.

One of the main themes of the study was that the majority of people who are long-term unemployed *want* to work. The preferred areas of work were office and factory work, although 8 per cent indicated that they wanted 'any kind of work'. The key advantages perceived with having a job included more income, opportunities for social interaction and teamwork, independence and confidence. The key barriers to gaining employment from the long-term unemployed people's perspectives were the cost of childcare, their lack of skills and experience, loss of benefits, and shortage of available job opportunities. Employers' attitudes to the long-term unemployed were also seen as a major barrier.

From the employers' perspective there was a preference for recruiting people with the necessary skills, rather than having to train them. They projected skills shortages in the information technology and hotel and catering sectors. An investigation into the recruitment methods used by employers showed that word-of-mouth is used extensively by small employers in particular. This may affect long-term unemployed people's chances of gaining employment. In areas of high unemployment there may be an entire community of people without employment. It is probable therefore that they would not have contacts in the workplace to recommend them for employment.

Employers' perceptions of the disadvantages of employing people who are long-term unemployed were interesting. Employers felt that the long-term unemployed would not have the skills for the particular jobs for which they would be recruiting. Other suggestions included that employers might not be able to depend on them as they could be 'lacking motivation', 'difficult to train', 'not interested in work' and 'difficult to integrate into the workforce'. One employer went so far as to describe them as 'social misfits'.

The project team's report, which included a number of key recommendations, was circulated to government representatives and agencies.

All of the team members looked forward to further involvement in projects of this nature. A follow-up study was, indeed, commissioned by the LES to examine proposed forms of support for employers in the area of recruitment and selection. Empowered team learning was used again.

Case-study 2

DESIGNING AND IMPLEMENTING A PERFORMANCE MANAGEMENT SYSTEM

The group was a loose association of companies in Ireland, the UK, Denmark and Holland which produced and marketed dairy and dairy-related products. The new group managing director wanted to create a sense of corporateness within the framework of a group strategy to replace the somewhat unco-ordinated and autonomous operations of the group's companies.

A newly developed corporate HR strategy was a critical component of the new style being introduced by the managing director and his top team. An important element of the HR strategy was the creation of a group-wide performance management system. Because of a tradition of independence from head office it was important that the system be designed and implemented in a way that would secure maximum buy-in and benefit to all managers in all parts of the group. An empowered team learning approach was adopted.

A team of six line and one HR manager was given the task of designing and implementing the new performance management system across the group. The key phases of the project were:

☐ an exploratory workshop
☐ consultation on the proposed specification for the performance management system
☐ a workshop to adapt the specification in the light of feedback and to design the system itself and plan necessary briefing and training
☐ training/briefing sessions
☐ planning the implementation
☐ review meetings.

The team came together for the first time at a workshop to explore the issues. The objectives were:

1 Develop in team members a shared understanding of the purposes and benefits of a performance management system, both to the company and to the individual.
2 Identify the benefits of objective-setting, as well as the consequences of not setting and reviewing objectives.
3 Agree the features of a process that would work well across the group.
4 Agree quality assurance standards.
5 Identify the enablers and blockers of an effective system of objective-setting and review.
6 Outline a proposed process for setting and reviewing objectives.
7 Agree whom to consult or check with before planning the implementation in detail.

The duration of the workshop was two days. Day one started with an exploration by the team of the concept of performance management. This was carried out by brainstorming the following questions:

□ *When you think of performance management, what words or phrases come to mind?*

□ *What are the possible purposes that can be served by a performance management system? Think in terms of benefits to the company and benefits to the individual.*

□ *What are the potential consequences for an organisation if it does not have an effective performance management system? Think both short- and longer-term.*

□ *In general how can we tell if a performance management system is working well?*

The second phase of the workshop focused on identifying and agreeing the characteristics of an effective performance management system for the group of companies. This was done by addressing the following questions:

□ *What features would you like to see in an effective performance management system across the group?*

□ *What things should we try and avoid?*

The specific ingredients of the objective-setting component of a performance management system were explored by brainstorming the questions:

□ *What are the potential benefits of effective objective-setting for (i) the individual, and (ii) the company?*

□ *What are the specific consequences of (i) not having formal objective-setting, and (ii) having an ineffective objective-setting process?*

The next step in the workshop was to identify the enablers and blockers to effective objective-setting across the group. This was done by brainstorming the following questions:

□ *In organisational terms, what are the factors or considerations that would help support and sustain an effective objective-setting system?*

□ *In organisational terms, what are the factors or considerations that would interfere with or undermine an effective objective-setting system?*

The team members jointly agreed the quality assurance standards in a proposed performance management system for the group by brain-storming:

☐ *What quality assurance standards would you like to see in an effective objective-setting system across the group?*

In the light of all the output obtained from these questions, the team set about the task of brainstorming and then agreeing the proposed standards for objective-setting in the group.

Day two opened with the task of specifying the proposed structure for a performance management system and the specific recommen-dations for a proposed objective-setting process. The team then planned a consultation process on the proposed structure for a per-formance management system, and the objective-setting component in detail, with the top management team and the project team's peers in all parts of the group. It did this by considering the following questions:

☐ *What do we want from the consultation?*
☐ *Whom do we need to consult?*
☐ *What do we want to ask them?*
☐ *What do we need to do to prepare?*
☐ *How will we know if we have been successful?*
☐ *Who sees whom, and when?*
☐ *What else do we need to think about to ensure that the consultation process is effective?*

The team then agreed the logistics of the consultation process and planned the remaining stages of the project. This was followed by a formal reflection and review on what individual members had learned and what the team had achieved during the course of the workshop.

The consultation document produced by the team started with the definition of a performance management system which the team had agreed at the exploratory workshop:

☐ A performance management system ensures effective implemen-tation of strategy to achieve the group's mission. It involves:
  – objective-setting
  – performance measurement and review
  – reward system
  – personal/career development.

The team saw the group mission and strategy as determining all the businesses' and hence individual managers' objectives. The project team saw the benefits of a performance management system as:

☐ a sense of common purpose

☐ achieving the desired results

☐ consistency across the group

☐ setting standards

☐ continuous development/improvement

☐ precise measurement and a sense of being in control

☐ better understanding and utilisation of human and other resources

☐ a loyal and motivated workforce

☐ a positive image internally and externally.

And it saw the benefits to the individual as:

☐ a clear understanding of what is expected in his/her role

☐ a better understanding of how the role contributes to the group's overall performance

☐ feedback on individual performance

☐ development to meet the demands of the role

☐ the opportunity to develop

☐ recognition and reward

☐ consistency and fairness

☐ motivation.

The team saw the process as cascading from the managing director down to the senior management team, through the businesses to departmental level, and ultimately to every employee. Objectives were to be set annually and reviewed regularly. The team proposed four phases of objective-setting:

1   clarification/discussion of strategy and agreement on critical areas

2   production of draft objectives

3   agreement on the objectives

4   regular reviews.

The team defined objectives as 'descriptions of what needs to be achieved by each individual to contribute to the overall success of the group and its people'. There are two kind of objectives:

☐ Role objectives are those that the role requires in order to achieve outcomes required by the appropriate level of strategy.

☐ Personal objectives are those that a person must achieve in order to succeed in the role and/or develop for future roles.

The team stressed that all objectives are ultimately dependent on the group mission, which is cascaded down through the organisation as different levels of agreed strategy. To emphasise this point a motto was offered by the Dutch member of the team which loosely translated as 'Everyone carries their own brick to build the wall.'

The team created its own quality standards for objectives – standards intended to –

☐ cover all critical areas in a role

☐ determine and focus an individual's priorities

☐ be realistic in terms of sphere of influence/control and resources

☐ be agreed, understood and written down

☐ be measurable by means of clear success indicators

☐ be reviewed regularly.

The team also proposed that 'wherever possible, objectives should also be motivating to the individual, and stretching and/or challenging.'

Following an extensive consultation across the company the team met again. The objectives of this two-day workshop were:

1 Agree the framework for the performance management system.
2 Design documentation and support material for objective-setting.
3 Agree the training/briefing needs for everyone involved.
4 Plan the implementation.
5 Celebrate the achievement.

Day one of the workshop covered:

☐ examining the findings and feedback from the consultation

☐ finalising the specification for the overall performance management system and for the objective-setting process

☐ a team learning exercise

☐ designing the documentation

☐ agreeing the quality assurance standards for objective-setting.

On day two the workshop focused on:

☐ specifying the training/briefing sessions

☐ practice at running the training/briefing sessions

☐ planning the rest of the project

☐ a final reflection and review.

The project team, with a few changes in its membership, then repeated the empowered team learning process to define and consult on reviewing performance and personal development planning across the group before implementing the agreed process. The project team repeated the process once more to define and implement the link between performance review and reward across the group. In this way empowered team learning was used to design and implement from the bottom up a performance management system that would be believed in and supported by everyone affected.

Case-study 3

OVERCOMING THE ISOLATION FELT BY OWNER-MANAGERS OF SMALL BUSINESSES

This section describes how a group of owner-managers of small businesses (SMEs) became a self-managing learning network. It recounts the experience of FASNET, a consortium of small businesses in Dublin.

The first step in the empowered team learning process was to invite owner-managers of SMEs in the Dublin area to attend a meeting to discuss the idea of setting up a learning network.

The objectives of the meeting were:

1 Develop a shared understanding of the benefits to be gained by SMEs' forming a learning network.

2 Discuss what could go wrong and how to identify success factors.

3 Think through and plan what should happen next.

The key objective at this stage was to enable the group to develop a shared understanding of what can be gained from a learning network.

The meeting began with introductions. The facilitator explained that his role was to facilitate and support the team in its discussion of networking, but not to endorse any specific viewpoint. The facilitator then reviewed the objectives of the meeting and explained that much of the group's thinking and decision-making would be carried out via a process of structured brainstorming. The facilitator referred the participants to questions on a worksheet and asked them (in pairs) to spend about 15 minutes writing down anything that came to mind.

□   *What benefits can be served by having a network?*
□   *What could go wrong?*

A third question was then posed by the facilitator:

□   *How will we know if a network is working successfully?*

This question encouraged the team to develop benchmarks that could be used later by network members to measure the quality and effectiveness of their meetings. The question also encouraged the team members to think of ways to overcome the problems that might be encountered by the network. A fourth question was then posed by the facilitator (again on a worksheet).

□   *What are the ways in which you can learn from each other?*

Sufficient time was allowed for generating and recording all the ideas within the group. Following discussion, the facilitator posed a final question.

□   *What do we need to think about to ensure that a network of this kind is a success?*

Considerations typically include:

□   objectives and goals for the network
□   the frequency of meetings, duration, location
□   other ways to interact
□   the structure of events and meetings
□   managing the process
□   the objective for the next meeting
□   information needed.

These questions encouraged the team members to plan ahead for the development of the network.

The final phase of the initial meeting was devoted to the team's setting its own agenda. The facilitator asked the members of the team to list what they would like to learn from a network of this kind. In this way the activities of the network and the support available could be directed towards meeting the members' needs.

The key outputs from the meeting were recorded on a flipchart and typed up for circulation prior to the next meeting. The potential benefits of forming and participating in a learning network were seen as

☐ sharing
  – our resources
  – information (eg about customers and markets)
  – our different areas of expertise
  – costs
☐ combining in order to
  – increase purchasing power
  – gain leverage (eg with banks)
  – build lobbying power
  – build new relationships
  – carry out promotional activity
  – trade together
  – avoid duplication
☐ learning together
  – to gain from experiences and lessons learned
  – to diagnose needs
  – and training together
  – in the joint use of consultants
  – in reconnaissance (eyes and ears, intelligence-gathering)
☐ mutual support
  – to have someone to turn to/talk to
  – to avoid isolation.

Things that could go wrong or undermine the effectiveness of a network were seen as:

☐ insufficient clarity of purpose
  – not having clear objectives
  – objectives not being shared by all members
  – not periodically reviewing objectives
  – feeling that the network is not there for all the members
  – regarding new members as diluting the sense of commitment
☐ inefficient management of the network
  – wasting time
  – varying levels of involvement/commitment by members
  – work being done by a small number

    – members not turning up or delivering what they agreed
    – breaches of confidentiality
    – overdependency on some members
    – loss of members
☐ not getting along together
    – personality clashes
    – lack of trust
    – domination by some members.

The next step was to develop an identity and a mission for the
new network. At this stage the group members began to realise
that they were in charge of the network, and that their commitment was required to make it work. The objectives of the workshop were:

1   Agree the formal objectives for the network.
2   Find a suitable name.
3   Discuss basic guidelines to maximise benefit for all members and
    prevent things going wrong.
4   Identify the criteria that would reveal if we are succeeding in our
    objectives.
5   Agree initial activities and time-scales.

The facilitator opened a discussion of the differences between an
organisation's mission, vision and values, and asked the members
about their individual company's mission statement.
    The facilitator then invited the network members to brainstorm
the following questions:

☐ *What makes a good mission statement?*
☐ *What makes a bad mission statement?*

The output from these questions was used to establish the criteria
against which the network's own mission statement would be generated and agreed. The output was collated and clustered into
broad categories. The team discussed and agreed the most important criteria. The team was then divided into three groups and each
drafted a mission statement on a separate flipchart. In plenary
session the agreed criteria were used to collapse the best
elements of the three draft statements into one agreed mission
statement.

The facilitator then referred the team to another question:

☐ *What might prevent us from being successful as a network?*

In the light of the output it generated, the team was then asked:

☐ *If these are the problems, what should we do to minimise or prevent them?*

Following plenary discussion and review, the team decided upon a set of principles that would guide its work and formulated them as the network's values.

The facilitator then moved the discussion on to creating a vision for the network. The process for eliciting and agreeing the vision was identical to the one used for creating the mission statement. By brainstorming what makes a good or bad vision, the team established the criteria against which they could create and evaluate the draft vision statement.

Having agreed the network's mission, values and vision, the team was now able to turn its attention to deciding on a name for the network. The facilitator asked:

☐ *In the light of our mission, vision and values, what name do we give ourselves?*

The mission, values and vision statements agreed by the FASNET members is shown below.

Our Mission

To share knowledge, expertise and experience that will strengthen all our people, and other resources, resulting in a more effective business.

We will do this by

☐ contributing participatively
☐ learning together
☐ exchanging commercial intelligence.

Our Values

We will

☐ be supportive of each other

☐ be open and truthful

☐ maintain confidentiality

☐ attend structured meetings with rotating roles

☐ work to mutually agreed standards and timetables

☐ expect to contribute to open and constructive discussion

☐ commit to our success.

Our Vision

For the next 12 months we will

☐ learn how to recruit staff more effectively

☐ be able to use effective techniques to improve the performance of employees and to develop their potential

☐ develop a mutual understanding of each other's businesses, visions, and markets

☐ exchange information on agreed subjects such as purchasing, pursuit of quality goals, market opportunities, labour law and industrial relations.

At the end of this session, members were asked to bring sufficient copies of their own company brochures, literature, etc, to the next meeting to enable all members to learn more about each other and to plan a presentation in any form that suited them. A database of network members was compiled for circulation to all the members.

The aim of this session was to strengthen the bond between team members by enabling them to get to know one another better. The sharing of company information helped to develop trust between the network members.

The objectives were:

1   Review the outputs of the previous meeting.
2   Present information on each member's company.
3   Get to know the other members better through reading their brochures, listening to their presentations and asking questions.

The facilitator presented the network's mission, values and vision on an overhead projector. The team broke into pairs to discuss what these statements meant in practice and how they would be guided by them. After 10 minutes the facilitator invited responses from each pair, and recorded them on a flipchart in the usual manner. Any changes to the network's mission, values and vision suggested as a result of this exercise were considered by the team. If agreed, the statements were subsequently modified.

The facilitator then initiated a discussion for the network members to get to know each other. The facilitator then introduced summary information on each company provided by the network members. Each network member was allocated a period of time to present his or her company in more detail to the rest of the team. During this period, company literature and brochures, etc, were circulated among the team.

The aim of the next meeting was to get network members to formally consider their learning and development needs. The output of this session was intended to provide a programme of topics and issues to be addressed at subsequent meetings.
The objectives were:

1   Prioritise the topics to be covered at network meetings.
2   Agree other issues for inclusion on the agenda.

The facilitator invited the group to draw up a list of questions under each of the key areas of interest it had identified. These key questions were then used to establish the current position of each of the member's companies with regard to each issue during an audit carried out on-site. The information for each company was summarised and integrated to see how it linked with the needs of other members. The information was collated and fed back to the team at the next session. The team used this information to plan the programme for the following six months.

A Pressing Problem Period (PPP) was a useful item for inclusion on the agenda at each network meeting. A member of the network presented a problem that was currently being experienced, and the other members made suggestions towards overcoming it. The pressing problems were specific to individual team members, but all the members benefited from talking them through and developing action options, based on their experiences.

The format for Pressing Problem Periods is outlined below.

☐   One team member volunteers to present a pressing problem at each meeting. The volunteer prepares a one-page form outlining the key features of the problem. The following questions may be used:

– Describe briefly the problem as you see it.
– What is the evidence to support your view?
– How long have you been aware of it as a problem, and what action have you taken so far?
– Are things a) getting worse, b) improving or (c) staying much the same?
– What do you think are the underlying causes of the problem?

☐ At the next meeting the designated speaker makes a presentation for 10 minutes, during which time the rest of the team listen and take notes if appropriate. The members of the group then ask questions for clarification.

☐ The team works in pairs to brainstorm possible action or solutions, which are recorded by the facilitator in the usual manner.

☐ The remainder of the session is spent discussing the problem firstly in pairs and then as a team, drawing on past experience and knowledge to arrive at useful solutions to solve the problem.

The facilitator may ask the person who 'owns' the designated problem to comment on the ideas in the light of what was experienced. When all extra ideas have been collected in the usual manner and discussed by the team, it may be useful to develop an action plan for the problem 'owner' to apply back to the workplace. Progress on the problem can be monitored and discussed in brief at subsequent meetings.

At this meeting the facilitator discussed personal development planning with the network members. The facilitator opened this discussion by presenting two questions to the group:

☐ *What possible purposes can be served by having a personal development plan?*

☐ *What are the possible consequences of not fulfilling your development plan?*

These two questions focused on the benefits of personal development. After 10 minutes' discussion in pairs, the facilitator collected in the responses in the usual manner. Following plenary discussion, participants were referred to two more questions:

☐ *What obstacles could prevent you from fulfilling your personal development plan?*

   ☐ *How could you overcome them?*

These questions encouraged the members to plan for any obstacles that might arise and to consider how they would deal with them effectively. Following discussion of these issues, the facilitator directed participants to three further questions:

   ☐ *In reaching your current work role, what do you consider to be*
       – your major achievements?
       – your greatest qualities?
   ☐ *What have been your*
       – biggest disappointments?
       – significant weaknesses?
   ☐ *What are your long-term plans? Where do you see yourself in three years?*

Team members were asked to assess where they were currently in their careers and where they would like to be. They were asked to consider the supporting and restricting factors that influence career development. They were encouraged to outline the activities required to promote their career development in the short and long term, and to consider how the learning network could assist them in achieving their goals.

    Self-management was an integral feature of the learning network. After six months in existence, the team members took stock of what had been achieved to date and what were the priority areas for the future.

    The objectives were:

1   Discuss how we are doing as a network.
2   Agree the best way forward.
3   Agree logistics.
4   Plan topics.
5   Review progress on initiatives.
6   Plan innovations.

The facilitator directed the members to consider the following questions:

   ☐ *What have you personally gained from membership of the network?*
   ☐ *What works well at network meetings?*

These questions helped the members to focus on evaluating their past experience of network meetings, including the logistics, and the topics covered. The facilitator recorded the responses and reviewed them on the flipchart. Following discussion, the facilitator then directed the team to consider two more questions:

☐ *In what ways could network meetings be improved?*

☐ *What topics would you like to have covered at future meetings?*

The team agreed on the priority areas for inclusion at subsequent sessions and for the future direction of the network. The facilitator then directed the network members to the final question:

☐ *What else could the network do to assist you in meeting your objectives?*

It may be necessary for the team to review its mission statement and to modify it over time in the light of what it has learned and achieved. This also serves the important function of providing focus for the future.

The objectives were:

1   Take stock of what has been achieved to date.
2   Review our mission and vision.
3   Decide on the issues to address at future meetings.
4   Plan the way forward.

Network members were asked to consider the following questions:

☐ *Looking back over the year since we came together, what for you personally have been the main benefits?*

☐ *What changes have you made in the way you (i) think about, and (ii) actually run your business?*

In FASNET, it was generally agreed that although a great deal had been learned during the first year, the value of attending meetings had declined in the second. There was a need for renewed focus on learning from each other, rather than trying to identify new topics or to widen membership of the group.

The objectives of the meeting to review the mission statement were:

1   Examine the mission with a view to revising it in the light of experience.

2 Revitalise the network meetings.

3 Decide how to get optimum benefit from the network.

The facilitator invited the team to consider its mission and to outline how they would achieve their aims by asking the network members to consider these questions:

☐ *What do you want to gain from the network in the next 12 months?*

☐ *In the light of the above, what changes do you suggest to the mission statement?*

The members worked in pairs to brainstorm the above questions. As a result a new mission statement was agreed by the members of FASNET:

Our Mission

To build on the trust that now exists within FASNET to learn as much as possible from each other's companies in order to benefit all our companies.

We will do this by
☐ a programme of visits to all the member companies and
   – listening
   – questioning
   – commenting
   – suggesting

with a view to contributing to the improvement of our business performance.

Through empowered team learning the network learned to be self-sufficient and continued in operation without the need of an external facilitator. By creating and re-creating its mission, the network had become self-managing.

CHANGING 'THE WAY WE DO THINGS ROUND HERE'

The company is committed to offering its customers and consumers a high-quality range of food products at fair prices. Its mission statement takes into account its employees, its shareholders and suppliers, and also gives consideration to being an upstanding member of the business community.

The management team decided that the company needed to become more customer-service-oriented and aimed to involve staff at all levels of the organisation in the change process. It decided to achieve this through empowered team learning.

The request for volunteers to join the project was so well received that too many people put their names down to be involved in the team itself.

The team had its first meeting to agree exactly what it was trying to achieve and how it was going to go about it. The team brainstormed the possible benefits of the project, and the main themes to emerge were:

☐ gaining trust

☐ giving the management committee a view of the way it really is

☐ understanding people's fears and concerns better

☐ learning new skills

☐ job security

☐ pride in and feeling part of the company.

The team also looked at the things that could go wrong in the process. The main themes to emerge from this brainstorming process were loss of credibility if things were not done in the right way; management's not taking the process seriously enough; that if communication was not carried through quickly people would lose faith; that people did not want change; and that people might even not want to be consulted.

The team members clarified what they wanted to get out of the consultation with their peers. They brainstormed ideas by asking the following questions:

☐ *What are the possible benefits or purposes of the consultation, assuming it is successful?*

☐ *What could go wrong in a consultation exercise of this kind?*

☐ *How might we tell that we were succeeding, during the consultation?*

□ *How will we feel if we are successful?*

As a result, the team arrived at its mission statement:

> To provide recommendations, as a result of consulting with everyone in the company, to the management committee that will help us to positively change the way we do things.

The team then set itself two additional aims:

□ by identifying the views of all employees on what needs to be done, to improve the processes, communications, teamwork, efficiency and morale in the company

□ to take the first steps in shifting the culture to one where people take responsibility, are highly motivated, feel that their knowledge and expertise are valued, feel part of a successful team, and, ultimately, perform at a level which delivers competitive advantage to the company.

The next step was for the team to decide how it was going to go about consulting everyone in the company. It did this by brainstorming the pros and cons of different methods of finding out what people think. The main methods considered were questionnaires, one-to-one interviews and group discussions. The team decided to carry out group discussions. The benefits of consulting in this way were that group discussions would be open to all, participation in them would be voluntary, and – perhaps most importantly of all – they were time-effective ways of gathering the information.

The team then brainstormed the range of issues that needed to be discussed in the group discussions, and agreed on four broad areas: processes, teamwork, morale, and other issues. The team then spent some time developing an understanding of what makes a good question, and of different kinds of questions.

The team spent the rest of the day practising and refining the skills of running group discussions. This was followed up by a second one-day workshop immediately before the group discussions were held.

The team decided that as many people as possible should be involved in the information-gathering, and that an effective communications process across the company would therefore be needed.

The team decided to send everyone in the company regular briefing notes providing updates on the team's progress, its plans, and a guide to when focus group discussions would take place. The first briefing note was sent out immediately after this first workshop. The briefing reported what had happened at the workshop and explained the rationale for wanting to change things; to some extent it was essentially a restatement of the things that had been said by the managing director in the kick-off meetings to invite people to take part in this consultation process. The team members decided to restrict discussion groups to a maximum of eight participants. Overall, approximately 200 staff participated in the discussions on a voluntary basis.

People involved in the early group discussions were very positive about the opportunity to participate: some of the planned two-hour sessions therefore lasted four hours during which everyone took a very active part. The positive experience of those people who took part in the process early on was shared among the rest of the site. Ultimately, therefore, the majority of people at the site took part in the discussions, despite the initial reluctance of some to do so.

The project team attended a two-day workshop to make sense of the findings. The workshop was designed to equip team members with the skills to collate, sort and analyse the information they had gathered. The project team was then able to identify the key themes coming out of the discussions, draw conclusions and prepare draft recommendations for consultation. Using quality standards which had been brainstormed and agreed at the initial workshops, each member of the team took responsibility for writing up the discussions. All of the results from nearly 20 different discussion groups were then collated.

At a three-day workshop the team learned the key skills of carrying out a contents analysis and analysed the data collated from all of the discussion groups. The team's analysis identified three key areas in which recommendations for change were required:

☐ the way work is organised
  – planning
  – staff levels
  – responsibility for decision-making
  – investment in equipment and tools of the trade
☐ the way we work together
  – teamwork between areas
  – lack of teamwork between the two sites
  – teamwork within areas

☐ morale

    − management attitudes
    − appreciation − the personal touch
    − insecurity − what is the long-term plan?
    − lack of information − leading to rumours.

The team also made recommendations on health and safety in the working environment, and on selection and development.

Immediately after the workshop, in order to communicate the findings, another briefing note was sent out to everyone in the company outlining the key issues that had come out of the consultation process. The briefing reassured people that none of the detail had been lost in the summaries. The briefing also clarified the next steps of the project which were to draw out the recommendations from the key issues identified, and to put these recommendations to the management committee.

The project team attended a one-day workshop to generate solutions. During this workshop the themes identified in the interpretation workshop were reviewed. The project team drew together the key suggestions for change in order to make recommendations for action and put together a presentation for the management committee.

The presentation to the management team was introduced as follows:

> Today we are here to communicate the views of all the people we have spoken to and recommend how we can improve things. We are here to help you understand the issues and recommendations by responding to your questions following the presentation.

The team members then summarised each of the key issues by identifying the problem, providing some of the examples that were quoted in the group discussions and providing some of the recommendations that were put forward in the group discussions to address it.

Overall, the employees believed that a general lack of planning, including contingency planning, was having an adverse impact on all company activities. Several examples were quoted and recommendations were made to review and improve planning of changeovers, stockholding, spare parts and levels of raw materials. The point was also made that there is a need to empower those who know of problems to recommend solutions and to be involved in decision-making.

The response to the work of the team was generally very positive. The vast majority of employees were very committed to the company.

There was a great anticipation of change and the team felt that having raised expectations it was important that it was now delivered. The recommendations would take some time to implement and it was important to identify some quick 'wins' in order to demonstrate progress quickly. The quick wins identified were to:

- □ establish a company newsletter
- □ announce a company-wide conference
- □ introduce a suggestion-box, with rewards
- □ produce a statement regarding plans for the manufacturing site over the next 12 to 24 months
- □ set up e-mail links with key customers
- □ re-establish team briefings
- □ announce a review of the planning process and set up a review team to do this.

In addition, a number of teams were set up to look at each of the detailed proposals more carefully and to put together an implementation plan. The empowered team learning process also resulted in significant personal development for project team members which was associated with a change in perceptions of their abilities and potential. Finally, in empowered team learning the company discovered a consultation process characterised by energy, creativity and commitment to change in most of the company's employees, and a deeper understanding of how to manage change.

In the next chapter we examine some of the management issues associated with empowered team learning.

7   MANAGING EMPOWERED TEAM LEARNING

Practical hints and tips

Empowered team learning is an exciting process. It taps into the creativity, energy, and responsibility that under the right conditions arise naturally in true teams where there is common purpose and shared mutual accountability. The benefits are not unique to empowered team learning but flow naturally from the evolution of the key steps of the method and the facilitation style. The facilitation is not essential throughout but it is helpful to groups for whom the level of responsibility that is critical to empowered team learning is unfamiliar, or to groups who could lose confidence early on and therefore forfeit the benefit of the later stages of empowered team learning.

Empowered team learning is applicable to any kind of team or group. It helps turn groups into teams in the true sense of the word. It also builds teams of any kind into skilful change agents. If there is a danger, it is that the experience of empowered team learning can raise expectations of a better or preferred way of working that is involving, highly participative, and democratic, in which people are not subordinated to the views of experts and other specialists or those in positions of power, and in which people have more control over their immediate environment.

It may be possible – and it should be one of the aims of empowered team learning – that the benefits of empowered team learning are retained and live on well beyond the scope of the original initiative. In some organisations, empowered team learning has been a trail-blazer; in others it has been used as reinforcement of wider organisational culture change. In and of itself, empowered team learning cannot change organisational cultures, but it can serve as a significant break with convention that can give support and confidence to those who believe that better results can be achieved through the empowerment of teams. Other things need to be in place to achieve lasting organisational culture change, but that is outside the scope of this book. Empowered team learning is an important foundation-stone although it is not the wall itself.

In this chapter we draw on our experiences of empowered team learning to identify practical hints and tips that could help potential sponsors or facilitators of empowered team learning. The following section is structured around the key steps of empowered team learning and contains practical guidance as well as highlighting the dangers and pitfalls

Winning organisational commitment to empowered team learning

At the very least the organisational sponsor needs to believe in the process sufficiently to give the go-ahead and to provide necessary support to the project team. The main benefits of empowered team learning can be summarised as:

☐ the fact that issues are analysed and solutions identified and implemented by a team made up of the key stakeholders – ie the people most directly affected by the issues under consideration

☐ a freshness of approach and associated language that is perceived to be open, honest and direct, and free from the jargon of experts, specialists or managers

☐ a level of trust in people which is rewarded with responsibility, maturity and loyalty

☐ the energy and innovation that stems from effective team learning and shared responsibility for outcomes

☐ growth in confidence and competence to learn, both as a team and as individuals

☐ a significant increase in shared understanding by members of the team of the wider organisational context and other perspectives

☐ the manifesting of an example to others of another way of working and of dealing with intractable organisational issues that people have learned to live with.

Rather than try to sell empowered team learning to sponsors, it is more effective if they are given an opportunity to experience some of the process in the manner described in Chapter 1. If at the end of the workshop the sponsors, having weighed up all the pros and cons, decide that empowered team learning is not appropriate, then that is clearly the right decision because the process will be seriously undermined without the support and understanding of management. Our experience is that once they have examined matters in this way, the sponsors often decide in favour of empowered team learning, if only because previous attempts to deal with the issue have either failed or have produced only limited results.

One advantage of gaining organisational sponsorship for empowered team learning is that the sponsors gain a deeper and shared understanding of what is involved and are thus better equipped to provide appropriate levels of support without interfering with the core process. If the group of organisational sponsors is representative of different parts of the organisation, even if they are not directly affected by the issue under consideration, the pilot workshop allows discussion of how empowered team learning could be a standard approach to dealing with complex issues. The pilot workshop can be used to explore the implications of a more democratic and participative style of team working across the organisation.

Forming the project team

The most important consideration when forming the team for empowered team learning is that the members should be representative of the key stakeholder groups, which can be highly localised to one area of the organisation or representative of the organisation as a whole. Ideally, there should be no one in a leadership role within the team, which should retain collective responsibility for its work and the outcomes. If managers are members of the team, they are there as individuals and not as formal or informal leaders of the team.

The team members need not be chosen for particular strengths and skills. It is more important that they are seen to be people who have a high degree of credibility with the groups from which they are drawn. The team's main authority and effectiveness does not result from its composition – ie its members – but rather from the authority that is progressively built up from its shared understanding of the issue and, crucially, from the information-gathering which is designed and carried out by the team.

Sometimes it is not appropriate to form a special team but to work with an existing team. The processes and method of empowered team learning are designed to equip any group of people with the confidence and competence to develop a shared understanding of a complex issue and to use systematic information-gathering to create and implement effective solutions.

It is important that the members chosen for the team are people who have a degree of standing and credibility with their peers. If the team is made up of people drawn from lower levels in the organisational hierarchy, it is important that they are not seen as management stooges. It can be helpful if some members are specifically chosen because they have strong views and are independent-minded. Instead of being disruptive, the empowered team learning process harnesses their contributions into the collective thinking of the team. This was particularly the case with the HGV drivers described in Chapter 1, among whom one of the team members was chosen because he was the former shop steward of the de-recognised union. His contributions were influential, but he eventually supported the collective view of the team, especially after the team's analysis of the results of the systematic information-gathering.

Another concern at this stage is the fear, on the part of the company, that the team is being given *carte blanche*. It is useful to make a distinction between objectives (or deliverables) and the remit of the team. The deliverables are the precise statement of what the team is being asked to bring about. The remit, by contrast, is a statement of how the team can go about achieving the objectives.

The deliverables and the remit set the boundaries for the team. They should be clearly defined as part of the briefing for the team, and should include clear statements of what the team is *not* being asked to achieve, if that helps clarify its objectives. The remit should always include a statement about designing, carrying out and interpreting the findings of some form of systematic information-gathering. If it is not appropriate to go outside the company to gather information, this should be stated at the outset.

As a guiding principle, the team should be given as much freedom as possible to plan and carry out its task. Too many imposed restrictions at the outset will lead the team to believe that empowered team learning is merely tokenism and that the team is not being entrusted with a serious task. The belief which evolves in gradually empowered team learning, that the team really is being trusted to carry out a task through to implementation, is crucial to a successful outcome.

Exploring the issues

The initial meetings and the exploratory workshop are critically important for the team members in enabling them to

- build the confidence to undertake the task without expert involvement
- learn that they can function without a formal leader
- understand the objectives and the remit
- establish between them an atmosphere of openness and trust among equals
- recognise that the team is working for its constituency and not for itself
- build up a shared picture of the wider context in which the team is operating
- recognise the importance of systematic information-gathering
- experience the power of a group process for examining issues and making decisions as a team.

Often when the teams meet for the exploratory workshop there is a strong feeling of fear that the absence of specialists or experts will lead to failure. Rather than deal with this issue directly, the facilitator encourages the team to start the process of examining its understanding of the objectives, the remit, and the issues the team has been asked to focus on.

The brainstorming of key questions and the systematic gathering in of all the ideas of the team members produce outputs that begins to make the team more confident about what it has undertaken. The just-in-time learning and gradual build-up of shared understanding and of the skills needed also help to overcome the initial fear of failure within the team.

Planning the information-gathering

It is important for the team to work with the level of information-gathering at which it feels comfortable. Later stages in empowered team learning provide the basis for the team to learn a simple but powerful method for extracting the main issues from the data collected without the involvement of complex and daunting statistics. As soon as statistical processing of the findings is involved the team members lose direct access to, and familiarity with, the data. The findings become not theirs but someone else's. The team members feel less confident to summarise the findings back to their peers and to enter into dialogue with them. The findings have become 'statistics' that in a sense belong to the 'experts' or in some sense to 'management'.

It is most important at this stage that the team does not lose confidence in its ability to carry out a systematic and comprehensive information-gathering exercise. It is for this reason that the team works out its own skill needs and satisfies them using the Learning Spiral. Too much theory at this stage could seriously undermine the collective innovation and decision-making by the group, making it feel that perhaps, after all, the information-gathering should be designed and run by others.

As with other key stages in empowered team learning, it is most important that neither the sponsors nor the team's facilitator try to influence the team's deliberations and thinking by injecting theory or guidelines created elsewhere. This is not to say that the team can work as slowly as it wishes, for it needs to work within the timetable it creates for itself in response to the remit which set the overall timescales. However, the team must be allowed to think things through, share ideas, and come up with its own guidelines, standards, working models, etc. To force the process by doing some of the thinking for the team undermines its confidence and its belief that it is empowered and able to achieve the objectives. The consequence is a loss of energy, creativity and drive, as well as reduced commitment to the overall objectives.

Collecting the information

The information-gathering phase can range from interviewing a small representative number of key stakeholders to running discussion groups with everyone in target populations. There is clearly an organisational commitment to the amount of time and other resources that need to be devoted to this stage. Unfortunately, it cannot be specified in detail in advance of commencing the empowered team learning process because it must be decided by the team, but only after the team has developed its shared understanding of the key issues.

In some ways there is an important act of faith on the part of the organisational sponsor. If too much is pre-decided on behalf of the team, the belief will develop in the team that it is not really in charge of the process, and that the strings are really being pulled by management. The likely scale of different kinds of information-gathering and the associated pros and cons of different options can be examined in the pilot workshop to secure organisational sponsorship, in exactly the same way as the team will examine the pros and cons in the exploratory workshop before deciding the nature and the scale of the information-gathering. Any constraints and boundaries can be incorporated into the remit.

Ideally, the team should carry out the information-gathering without external assistance, though a number of interim review meetings are essential.

Making sense of the findings

This is often the hardest phase for the team. Up to this point the team has grown in confidence, and there is sometimes a feeling of excitement and elation that it has been entrusted with a task of key importance to the organisation. The exploration of ideas, the build-up of shared understanding, and the information-gathering itself, even though it can be daunting, is on the whole enjoyable and rewarding for the team members. The hard grind of data collation and summary can come as a bit of a shock, as can the realisation that the team members have to be, and be seen to be, impartial and objective with the findings. On the other hand, the impact of the wide range of responsibility that lies with the team is balanced by the growing awareness of the insights, knowledge and understanding of the team members.

The introduction of formal statistical treatment of the findings – other than the process used in the workshop described in Chapter 5 – to make sense of the findings, can undermine the overall benefits of empowered team learning, because there is a loss of ownership by the team of its own findings.

It is important that the sponsors or other managers in the organisation do not attempt to gain foresight of the findings by asking for an interim report or presentation, because once again the team will feel that it is not in control of the process or that the members are not being trusted.

Checking back

The checking- or summarising-back phase is crucial to the overall success of empowered team learning because it provides reassurance to the team that it has correctly captured what the people involved in interviews and group discussions said. It also provides reassurance to the stakeholder groups that the team is working on the authority of the data rather than solely on its own thinking. This helps build confidence in the work of the team and in the empowered team learning process. It is most important that the checking-back phase is not abandoned or only done half-heartedly, because that would seriously undermine the effectiveness of empowered team learning. In addition, the enrichment of the team's thinking from the feedback would also be lost.

Finding a solution

Finding a solution can be demanding and potentially frustrating for the team. As in the exploratory workshop, skilful facilitation is essential, or the confidence of the team that it can see the process all the way through to a successful outcome will be reduced. The team must not be protected from the 'pain' of creation by letting go of, or short-circuiting, the process, nor by offering solutions not thought of by the team itself, nor by pushing new ideas and suggestions into the arena that come from the facilitator or the sponsor or other outsiders.

The key message here is: trust the process! If all the previous steps of empowered team learning have been followed to this point, and the key workshops facilitated in the manner described in Chapter 5, then the team is capable of finding its own solutions. The energy, the shared understanding from its discussions, the enrichment of that thinking from the analysis of the data gathered, and the acquired sense of responsibility for the outcome all combine to equip the team to find appropriate solutions.

If the workshop does not result in a clear way forward for the team, it may be necessary to meet again, starting with a fresh look at the main conclusions from the information-gathering. In our experience, a team following the empowered team learning process has never needed more than two workshops to arrive at a set of recommendations that has the full commitment and support of every member of the team.

This is the phase that some sponsors are most nervous of because they fear that the recommended solution will be unrealistic, irresponsible or unreasonable. In practice the outcomes of empowered team learning are usually highly responsible and realistic because the viewpoint and perspectives of key stakeholders have been assessed and taken into account by the people who have a vested interest in making the recommendations work.

Consulting, getting buy-in, and planning the implementation

Having worked out its solution or the planned actions, the project team designs and carries out formal consultation sessions with key stakeholders with a view to securing their support and acceptance of the planned action.

If the initial team knows that it will have responsibility for implementing the solution it proposes (whether or not the solution has to be sanctioned or approved by others), it is less likely to make recommendations that it does not wholeheartedly believe in. Equally, it is more likely to have examined all the pros and cons carefully because it will have to live with the consequences of its actions. In general, empowered team learning is less effective if all the team has to achieve is a set of recommendations.

Because of the time involved, it is often not possible to allow all the members of the team to continue all the way through to a successfully evaluated outcome. An effective compromise is to have a periodic change in the membership of the team. In this way the team does not lose momentum and gains from periodic additions of new blood. However, great care has to be taken in induction and bringing new members up to speed. This should be done by immersing new members in the normal processes of the team for sharing ideas and making decisions, rather than through formal briefings.

There is relatively little 'selling' involved because the stakeholder groups have been closely involved throughout the process. Feedback from the checking-back sessions and also the consultation sessions is critical not only in enriching the thinking of the team but also in progressively achieving buy-in and support from the wider group of stakeholders. Planning the implementation is relatively straightforward if all the preceding steps in empowered team learning have been successfully completed.

Briefing, reviewing, and monitoring meetings

The briefing phase should come as no surprise because of the close involvement of stakeholders in earlier stages of empowered team learning. The reviews and monitoring are crucial to ensure that the implementation plans are working and that the performance indicators agreed by the team are being recorded and evaluated. It is most important that they are not omitted as an unnecessary luxury because they strongly contribute to maintaining the level of ownership and commitment that empowered team learning achieves.

Designing for success: some guiding principles

Taken as a whole (see Figure 7) empowered team learning achieves successful outcomes where responsibility is given to a representative stakeholder team which is progressively equipped by means of systematic information-gathering and

Figure 7
FACTORS CONTRIBUTING TO THE EFFECTIVENESS OF
EMPOWERED TEAM LEARNING

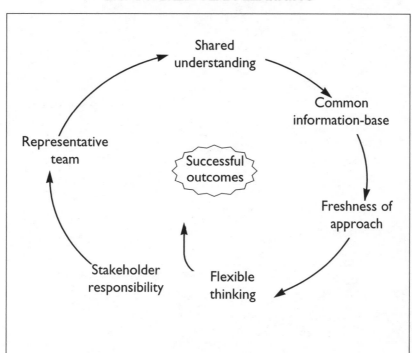

the evolution of a shared understanding to bring fresh thinking to an issue of concern to the members of the team.

The key empowered team learning workshops are designed to develop confidence and competence in the team on a just-in-time learning basis to develop shared understanding within the team. The information-gathering critical to empowered team learning creates a common information-base, the validity of which is tested in the checking-back sessions, and results in a sense of authority or confidence within the team. This, when combined with the shared understanding within the team, encourages the freshness of approach and the flexible thinking that leads to innovation, creativity and the feasibility of the solutions generated by the team.

Figure 8
**FACTORS UNDERMINING THE EFFECTIVENESS OF
EMPOWERED TEAM LEARNING**

Unrepresentative
team

Restricted Remit

Ownership of issue
lies elsewhere

Partial or
short-lived
solutions

Variable
understanding

Key decisions/analysis
dependent on
others

Incomplete or biased
information-base

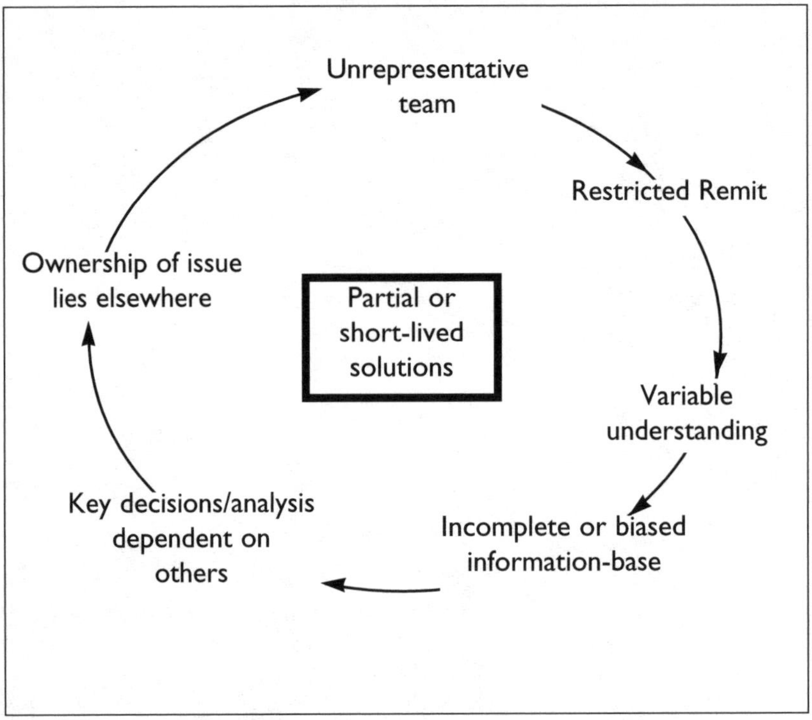

By contrast, the factors that undermine the effectiveness of team learning are the same as the factors which typically result in partial or short-lived solutions common to many change programmes (see Figure 8).

Variations on a theme: the core method and possible variations

At the heart of empowered team learning is the gradual acquisition of the credibility and the authority to deal with complex issues by a group of people not normally entrusted with such tasks. In Chapter 3 we discussed the factors that underlie the success of empowered team learning. The group that forms the project team must be representative of the key 'coalface' workers who are most directly affected by the issues being addressed.

The team is not led and is not supported by experts or

specialists other than the process facilitator. The team must be granted, and also develop, a high degree of responsibility for, and control over, the outcomes. The team must progressively build a shared understanding of key issues and acquire the skills it needs on a just-in-time basis. Critically, the team must carry out some form of systematic information-gathering and be completely responsible for analysing and interpreting the findings with no outside help other than from the processes facilitator.

In some of the cases we described earlier in this book (eg the HGV drivers, and the food company) the team's remit required them only to make a set of recommendations to senior management at the end of the process. If the team believes that it is being trusted to carry out an important task without outside interference or regular progress checks from the sponsor, then the means by which the recommendations have been reached, using empowered team learning, should ensure that they are balanced, reasonable and accurately reflect the thinking of everyone who contributed to the study. Surprises for the sponsor are unlikely, other than perhaps the sheer quality of thinking and the richness of the ideas. Empowered team learning achieves a sense of dialogue between relevant groups where respective viewpoints are recognised and understood.

In other cases described in this book (eg the safety initiative in the refinery) the team's remit included full implementation and evaluation of the outcomes, with the management group as one among several key players in the overall process, rather than as a hurdle that the team had to overcome before it moved from one step of empowered team learning to another. In our view, the best results are achieved this way, but it is not always possible in practice.

The importance of self-defined performance indicators

In the spirit of giving the team as much responsibility for its own thinking and actions as possible, the formulation by the team of its own success and performance indicators at the outset and at key stages is critically important. The questions posed by the facilitator at different points in empowered team learning usually take the form:

□ *How might we tell if we are being successful?*

□ *What would indicate to us that we have achieved the deliverables?*

□ *What would indicate to others that we are being successful?*

These questions are posed in relation to the project as a whole (and periodically reviewed) and also to key phases or activities.

Making explicit the team's collective thinking about the evaluation of outcomes, as well as the ongoing evaluation of key stages, is critically important to the success of empowered team learning. Responsibility for ongoing and endpoint evaluation should ideally lie with the team itself. This responsibility should not be deferred to others.

Believing in and trusting the process

Several times through the course of this book we have stressed the importance of believing in and trusting the process. It is crucial that the sponsor understands how the process needs to evolve or there is a danger of the team's being too closely monitored and checked up on. If this happens, the team is likely to lose confidence that it really is being trusted to deliver the outcomes, and cynicism and disenchantment will set in, and there may possibly even be some form of subversion.

There are times when the team will struggle and may even feel frustrated. The easy solution would be to help the team by offering direction or answers to the issues that the team is struggling with. It is most important that the team is allowed to find its own solutions and develop its own thinking collectively. Part of the skill of the facilitator lies in an ability to allow the team to struggle at times and learn to cope with a sense of frustration rather than to protect the team from discomfort which can result in a loss of shared responsibility.

Honesty pays

This may seem a naive heading but openness and honesty in terms of expectations and also limitations and boundaries in terms of the team's remit are important to the success of empowered team learning. It is usually better for the sponsor to be honest about limitations and boundaries at the outset rather than to imply that there is more freedom and responsibility than there actually is. It is important to establish this point, ideally by means of the sponsor's initial workshop, where the fuller understanding of empowered team learning that is developed usually gives the sponsor greater confidence in the process and also the confidence to be open and honest about limitations and boundaries.

The team will be more motivated by an honestly restricted remit within which it is given full responsibility than a fuller remit that is actually misleading.

Overcoming the fear

Especially when working solely with people who are completely unaccustomed to working in this way, it is important to recognise the strong element of fear-of-failure or fear-of-being-shown-up-as-ignorant that will affect many of the team members. Even with groups of line managers, the absence of specialists and experts can be unnerving. The key point is not that experts should not be used as part of empowered team learning but that they should not form part of the team and should not be given a formal role to advise and guide the team.

The team should first of all develop its own thinking assisted by the process facilitator. In this way the natural desire to rely on experts is radically reduced. If access to experts is needed, the team is better equipped to use experts as a flexible resource because of the deepened shared understanding of issues created by empowered team learning. In the example described in Chapter 1 the HGV drivers had never planned or run a survey before, had never interviewed their own managers, and had never planned and carried out a formal presentation to the senior management team before – to name just a few of the firsts that were notched up during the course of the project. The unfolding of the empowered team learning process and the facilitation process used in the workshops cumulatively help to overcome the natural fears and misgivings felt by team members. The gradual recognition by the individual team members that everything is collectively done also helps overcome individual fears.

Different aspects of empowered team learning help individual team members in different ways to overcome their fears. Our experience is that the fears and concerns die away quickly as the team members experience the process as powerful and enjoyable. Nonetheless the sponsors should recognise how easily the pride and sense of achievement can disappear if due recognition and acknowledgement for achievement is not given.

Choosing the facilitator

It is evident that the role of the facilitator is crucial to the success of empowered team learning. Sufficient detail has been given in the case-studies for a skilled facilitator not only to know what happened but also how it was achieved, especially in the key workshops. Chapter 3 explains the process and Chapter 5 gives detailed guidelines on the five key workshops. It is important to remember that empowered team learning is a not a system that is followed slavishly. It is a method with key steps and some powerful underlying guiding principles. The facilitator does not need to follow the detailed workshop facilitation notes in Chapter 5 if in his or her judgement the same output can be achieved by other processes which work just as well, so long as the approach is consistent with the principles underlying empowered team learning.

It is critically important that the facilitator genuinely believes that ordinary people can be empowered to achieve some of the kind of results described in this book. Without this belief it will be difficult for a facilitator to make the fine adjustments or the myriad process decisions needed to get the best out of the team.

Empowered team learning as the norm

All the cases described in this book were projects carried out either by existing or by specially formed teams, in most cases with a clear beginning, middle and end, though in some cases the end became the beginning of an ongoing process that involved the successors to the original team. The team members have usually enjoyed the process and experienced the power of participative democratic working that lies at the heart of empowered team learning. Several team members have raised the question 'Why is this the exception rather than the norm? Why can't this way of working be the way we address all our concerns and problems?'

It is not always easy to find convincing explanations that justify the continued preoccupation of most organisations with top-down, management-led solutions on issues that affect everyone in the organisation. Systems designed by outside experts or consultants, and change programmes that are conceived and led by people who are remote from the world as it is experienced by those for whom the programmes are designed, often result in only superficial and short-lived change.

Empowered team learning was conceived as a method for tapping into and harnessing the collective knowledge and understanding of representative stakeholder groups in a process that deliberately shifts responsibility for outcomes away from senior managers, team leaders, experts or specialists. The process could not be used completely to plan and specify the design of a nuclear energy plant, though it could advantageously be used to tackle many of the issues surrounding the design of the human-system interfaces.

There is a gradual move away from monolithic hierarchical organisations that are physically embodied in office or manufacturing sites towards virtual organisations that are manifested in the constant forming and re-forming of networks, both physical and electronic. Empowered team learning might acquire a more natural fit in a new form of work organisation in which it becomes the norm rather than the exception in the way the more intractable and complex issues facing human beings at work are dealt with and resolved.

RESOURCE

Theoretical underpinnings: what we know about learning in teams

This section is offered as a resource to those who want an objective summary of current thinking in the published theoretical and research literature on the subject of team learning.

The summary has been broken down into the following six areas:

1 what is team learning?
2 processes of team learning
3 structural contexts influencing team learning
4 individual skills which facilitate team learning
5 social contexts which impact on team learning
6 optimising team learning.

What is team learning?

Team learning can be defined as the way in which teams learn collectively. In order to develop a true understanding of 'team learning' we reviewed the meanings associated with its composite words 'learning' and 'team' and the published research on teams and collective learning.

Psychologists have been developing theories of individual learning for over a hundred years, and philosophers for centuries before that. One approach which strives to integrate this vast body of knowledge is that of Crossan *et al* (1994). They argue that learning involves changes in both cognition and behaviour, and that changes in one may precede changes in the other. Integrated learning is the result of both cognitive and behavioural changes – where neither occurs, no learning has taken place.

There is a body of work based around the idea that adults learn differently from children. According to Knowles (1987), adult learning theory holds that:

□ Adults learn differently from children and have different

needs and motivating factors in learning situations.

□ Adults need to be responsible for their learning experiences.

□ Adult learners should be involved in developing their learning materials.

□ Once adults see a reason to learn, they will participate actively and creatively in the learning experience.

□ Adults should be allowed plenty of practice time.

□ Competencies learned should be linked to the adult learner's ability to perform work better.

□ Learning should be linked to the adult learner's previous experiences – eg learning by analogy.

There is a rapidly growing literature on organisational learning, which is too large to summarise here. One noteworthy review has identified three areas of consensus about organisational learning (Fiol and Lyles, cited by Danau and Sommerlad, 1996):

□ the importance of environmental alignment

□ the distinction between individual and organisational learning

□ the presence of four key contextual factors:
   – culture
   – strategy
   – structure
   – environment.

David Schwandt (1996) emphasised the distinction between the dimensions of performing and learning. For any task there are two key dimensions – doing it, and learning how to do it better. Most research has focused on one dimension or the other, rather than seeking to integrate the learning and performing dimensions. Mary Crossan *et al* (1994) did, however, examine the link between learning and performance in their research. They highlight an important paradox: if you accept that failure helps learning, then learning cannot be simply defined as performance improvement. The implication is some learning must result in failure for further learning to occur.
  It is relatively straightforward to conceptualise teams in

broad terms – for example, 'groups of people that work together cohesively towards a common goal' (Dechant *et al*, 1993). However, typologies of teams suggest that the notion of a team is not so straightforward in practice.

Ungar and Lorscheider (1996) identify three different types of group/team in the workplace:

☐ work teams
☐ integrating teams
☐ improvement teams.

Hackman (1986) suggests a more complex typology of teams:

☐ top management
☐ task forces
☐ professional support groups
☐ performing groups
☐ human service teams
☐ customer service teams
☐ production teams.

As Ungar and Lorscheider's (1996) review suggests, 'There is no generally accepted and integrative theory of groups.' Although a vast quantity of research has been conducted into the areas of individual and organisational learning, group/team learning appears to have fallen between the gap in these two levels and escaped significant attention.

The work of Senge *et al* (1994), Dechant *et al* (1993), Argote and McGrath (1993) and others has, however, given us some insight into the relationship of team learning with more commonly researched team issues including:

☐ team innovation
☐ group effectiveness
☐ group dynamics
☐ co-operative learning and education
☐ team decision-making
☐ distributed cognition.

Team learning is critical to teambuilding, to team performance and to the improvement of team performance. Team learning links performing and learning, which includes the way teams select their vision and goals. Senge (1994) describes this process as 'alignment': 'Building alignment is about enhancing a team's capacity to think and act in new synergistic ways, with full co-ordination, and a sense of unity.'

Processes of team learning

The processes which take place within a team can have a significant effect on its ability to learn. Argote and McGrath (1993) conducted a major review of group processes and identified four major types:

☐ construction – the formation and development of groups

☐ operations – doing what the group does

☐ reconstruction – embedding new knowledge

☐ external relations – monitoring and managing the group's relation to its embedding systems.

Construction processes are the activities in the initial establishment of a group in an organisational context, such as recruitment, socialisation and definition of purpose.

Dechant *et al* (1993) categorise group development models into three types: progressive, cyclical, and non-sequential. Progressive models assume that group processes and performance improve over time. The classic 'forming, storming, norming and performing' model falls into this category. Cyclical models adopt a life-cycle approach, differing from the progressive models in describing the 'death' of a group as a natural part of its evolution. Non-sequential models hold that group development depends on the group's context, characterised by factors such as task process activities, relations, and focus.

Dechant *et al* (1993) described team learning in terms of a cyclical model of team development, outlining each stage a team must pass through in moving towards the synergistic type team learning defined by Senge *et al* (1994). The four stages of their model include:

☐ *fragmented learning* – Learning has not moved beyond the individual and is inhibited because members hold different frames.

☐ *pooled learning* – Clusters of individuals learn within the group, but there is little collective reframing.

☐ *synergistic learning* – Meaning schemes are altered or discarded as a result of collective reframing among group members.

☐ *continuous learning* – All team learning processes are used easily and regularly. Collective reframing has become the norm. Members' perspectives are easily integrated and evolved into consensual understanding. The group has developed the habit of seeking out and valuing diversity, internally and externally, in order to broaden its perspective. The team experiments, often – individually and collectively – within the larger organisation, thus extending learning to others.

Operations processes are ways in which groups work to achieve their core purpose in organisations. Argote and McGrath (1993) identified four modes in which groups can work:

☐ the inception of a project
☐ the solution of technical issues
☐ the resolution of conflict
☐ the execution of the performance requirements of the work.

Reconstruction processes involve groups' using their operations activities as a basis for modifying themselves or learning. They are therefore of particular relevance in understanding how teams learn.

Because most group research is conducted on a short-term basis, and 'these reconstruction processes do not show up until one is dealing with a group that has some meaningful history, some continuation over time' (Argote and McGrath, 1993), there is a lack of research in this important area.

The group learning curve refers to the widely observed phenomenon that performance or output improves over time.

Economists have long used this model at the level of organisations, but Argote applied the concept to teams. Argote *et al*
(1995) found that groups who do not experience a change of
membership are more productive than groups that do change.
The difference in productivity was greater for simple tasks
than for complex tasks, supporting the view that the observed
learning curve in complex tasks is due to *innovation*, rather
than *repetition* of the task.

Crossan (1994) has identified four key processes in group
learning to make up the '4I learning framework':

☐ *intuiting* – the development of new insights
☐ *interpreting* – the development of insights into more
   clearly defined ideas
☐ *integrating* – the shared understanding of an interpretation
☐ *institutionalising* – the embedding of individual and group
   learning into organisational artefacts such as systems,
   structures, and procedures.

Ungar and Lorscheider (1996) identified a hierarchy of moti-
vational levels for learning in groups:

☐ being allowed
☐ knowing how
☐ knowing why
☐ wanting.

Brookes (1994) and Dechant *et al* (1993) argue that the following key aspects of the adult learning process also apply to
the team learning process:

☐ *framing* – the group's initial perception of something,
   based on past understanding and present input
☐ *reframing* – the process of transforming a perception or
   frame into a new understanding
☐ *experimenting* – the testing of hypotheses
☐ *crossing boundaries* – the communication and movement
   of ideas and information between and among people
☐ *integrating perspectives* – the synthesis of divergent views
   so that apparent conflicts are resolved through dialectical
   thinking, not compromise or majority rule.

In Dechant *et al*'s systems model of team learning, these processes are seen to integrate thought and action. Framing and reframing processes are about thinking, integrating perspectives brings together thinking and action, and crossing boundaries and experimenting is about the group's subsequent action.

The way in which teams manage their external relations is another important issue. This covers the way in which groups acquire knowledge about the environment, how knowledge is transferred, and the way teams respond to environmental threat or uncertainty. Gladstein-Acona (1987) concludes that: 'Group process includes the intra-group and intergroup actions that transform resources into a product. Process includes both the way in which group members interact with one another and the way in which they interact with those outside the group's boundaries.'

Structural contexts influencing team learning

Team learning is also affected by the context in which a team operates. The contextual factors which can influence team learning fall into three categories:

☐ team task
☐ organisational context
☐ team context.

Learning in teams is likely to be affected by the type of task being carried out by the team. Argote and McGrath (1993) break down the types of tasks teams carry out in order to meet the performance requirements of their work into:

☐ planning tasks
☐ creative tasks
☐ intellective tasks
☐ decision-making tasks
☐ cognitive conflict tasks
☐ mixed-motive tasks
☐ competitive tasks
☐ performance/psycho-motor tasks.

In setting the scene for optimal team learning, the contexts of these different types of tasks should be taken into account.

Teams also operate within the wider context of organisations. The four key factors that influence organisational learning, highlighted by Fiol and Lyles (cited by Danau and Sommerlad, 1996), are:

☐ culture
☐ strategy
☐ structure
☐ environment.

The context established at the organisational level will influence the way in which teams learn. Contextual factors within a team or group itself can then also impact on team performance. Danau and Sommerlad (1996) identify some 'natural properties' of groups which may impair the ability of people in teams to learn collectively in an effective way:

☐ conformism
☐ risky shift
☐ group-think
☐ double loyalty
☐ lack of facilities and 'action space'.

King and Anderson (1990) review several antecedents of innovation in work groups including:

☐ leadership
☐ cohesiveness
☐ group longevity
☐ group composition
☐ group structure.

Studies have found that a democratic, collaborative leadership style encourages group innovation. One study found that 'highly innovative teams exhibited a higher degree of leadership support, goal emphasis, teambuilding and work facilitation' (West and Wallace, 1988). However, it is noted that this research has not considered other factors, and more research is needed on the kinds of group environments that encourage innovation before recommending how leaders may influence groups to be innovative.

The research literature suggests that cohesiveness can have two contradictory influences. Cohesiveness can encourage innovation because it increases team members' feelings of self-actualisation and psychological safety. However, cohesiveness is strongly linked to group homogeneity. People in homogeneous groups are unlikely to question group decisions, and likely to focus on relationships rather than tasks – potentially leading to the group-think phenomenon (Janis, 1982). Low cohesiveness may be beneficial early in the process of producing creative ideas, and high cohesiveness may help groups to implement innovations successfully.

Research has suggested that people are more innovative when groups have a relatively short lifespan. One study is cited which found longevity to be negatively related to performance in research and development teams. However, the impact of longevity is not so clear cut: innovation and performance are not the same thing, and longevity is likely to be linked with cohesiveness.

Group composition includes aspects such as size and the personalities of individual team members. Teams need one or two opinion leaders to disseminate the team's work, as well as one or two people to play the role of 'devil's advocate'. This has been shown to lead to more options being examined by team members, and therefore, potentially to better-quality decisions.

Research has shown that groups with 'organic' structures (an integrative, team-based approach to tasks, blurred boundaries of authority and influence, professional commitment) are more innovative in their approach to group tasks.

Campion *et al* (1996) describe a useful model of the relation between work team characteristics and team effectiveness, as measured by productivity, satisfaction and manager judgements. The framework is shown below:

- □ job design
  - self-management
  - participation
  - task variety
  - task significance
  - task identity

- □ interdependence
  - – task interdependence
  - – goal interdependence
  - – interdependent feedback and rewards
- □ composition
  - – heterogeneity
  - – flexibility
  - – relative size
  - – preference for teamwork
- □ context
  - – training
  - – managerial support
  - – communication and co-operation between teams
- □ process
  - – potency (belief that the team can be effective)
  - – social support among the members
  - – workload-sharing
  - – communication and co-operation within the team.

Wellins *et al* (1991) also identify six key factors in team development processing:

- □ commitment
- □ trust
- □ purpose
- □ communication
- □ involvement
- □ process orientation.

Individual skills which facilitate team learning

A team is made up of a collection of individuals who all bring with them skills that might facilitate or hinder collective learning. Some of the skills that could help people learn effectively in teams include dialogue skills, skills of learning sets, skills frameworks, skills of leading learning teams, and a framework of group behaviours.

Senge *et al* (1994) identify dialogue skills – the skill of balancing enquiry and advocacy – as important for effective team learning. Dixon (1994) has identified some of the specific skills required: to provide others with accurate and complete information, to confirm others' personal competence when disagreeing, to make explicit the reasoning that supports a position, to express the perspective of others, to change position when others offer convincing data, to regard assertions as hypotheses to be tested, and to challenge errors in others reasoning by using data.

Cunningham (1994) provides the following guidelines for effective team meetings:

- ☐ Accept responsibility for your own learning.
- ☐ Collaborate with others in their learning, but do not try to take it over for them.
- ☐ Listen actively to everyone.
- ☐ Do not try to make people be like you – accept them as they are.
- ☐ The details of what happens are confidential.
- ☐ Try to be as open and honest as possible.
- ☐ Everyone has the right to a reasonable amount of the group's time.
- ☐ Try to present honest concerns.
- ☐ Speak for yourself: use 'I'.
- ☐ Everyone has the right not to answer a question.
- ☐ Agreed rules apply to team facilitators/leaders too!
- ☐ Decisions are taken collectively by consensus.

Wellins *et al* (1991) propose that the different types of skills needed by empowered teams fall into three categories:

- ☐ team/interaction skills
- ☐ quality/action skills
- ☐ job skills (highly job-dependent).

The specific skills in each of these categories are summarised below:
- ☐ team/interaction skills:
  - – listening and feedback
  - – one-to-one communication
  - – handling conflict
  - – influencing others

- training job skills
- team skills (participating in meetings)
- working in teams

☐ quality/action skills:
- clarifying (internal and external) customer requirements
- identifying improvement opportunities
- developing and selecting solutions
- planning the improvement
- ensuring ongoing quality

☐ job skills (highly job-dependent):
- equipment operation
- safety practices
- maintenance basics
- production processes.

These categories are supported by Danau and Sommerlad's (1996) review in which they identify the competency requirements for team working as:

☐ technical, functional or job competences

☐ team, interactive, interpersonal and communication competencies

☐ action, problem-solving and decision-making skills.

Hackman (1986) has identified five common mistakes, or 'tripwires', made by leaders of learning teams:

☐ calling the performing unit a team, but managing members as individuals

☐ falling off the authority balance beam

☐ assembling a large group of people, telling them in general terms what needs to be accomplished, and letting them work out the details

☐ specifying challenging team objectives, but skimping on organisational supports

☐ assuming that members have all the competence they need to work well as a team.

Social contexts which impact on team learning

As Crossan *et al* (1994) point out, team learning is a fundamentally social activity, and as such it is far more than the simple transmission of information. In reality 'they may not see it until they believe it' because learning is impacted by different social contexts.

Levine, Resnick and Higgins (1993) highlight the need to consider thinking as a form of social interaction and outline five key areas for consideration:

□ the presence of others
□ social roles, positions and identities
□ the mental representations of others
□ social interaction and cognitive change
□ cognition as collaboration.

Schwandt (1996) builds on the work of Parsons to identify four learning subsystems. Each of these subsystems represents a function that must be implemented in order for an organisation (or a team) to learn:

□ *environmental interface* – activities which lead to the two-way flow of information across the team's boundaries
□ *action/reflection* – examination of the results of actions, enabling the team to develop new knowledge
□ *structuring* – acts of communication, networking and co-ordination, and roles supporting the movement of information and knowledge
□ *meaning and memory* – a set of shared schema that permit, enhance, or exclude information or knowledge flow.

A balanced combination of the action/reflection and meaning and memory subsystems is particularly important if a team's learning is to be a continual process.

Dixon (1994) identifies four conditions which enhance the collective interpretation of information:

□ information and expertise are distributed
□ egalitarian values
□ the organisation's size and physical arrangement supports frequent interactions between subsystems
□ processes and skills that support organisational dialogue are in place.

Brookes (1994) notes the important role of power differentials between team members: 'In order to remake the culture of the organisation, power differences among team members must not simply be controlled – they must be eliminated. Such power differences result in the exclusion, rather than the integration, of multiple perspectives and thus severely limit the learning that is possible by teams in work organisations.'

McKenna (1995) draws on chaos theory, and the proposition that 'what happens in an organisation has sensitive dependence on initial conditions'. 'These initial conditions are usually the result of political interaction between people within the organisation, based on the initial ability of individuals to deal competently with one another.' He points out that 'This is not a free-for-all display of feelings and emotions but a disciplined attempt to test the un-discussable matters that could be blocking the learning process.'

Optimising team learning

The information available on team learning, its processes, and the structural contexts, individual skills and social contexts which influence it, can be integrated to suggest ways of optimising the team learning process. Indeed, it highlights ten key areas that need to be taken into consideration and manipulated if optimal collective learning conditions are to exist.

1: The way adults learn
Research on adults reveals that they learn differently from children. The chief implication of this research is that teams should be encouraged to take charge of their learning and the way it is achieved. Teams should also be equipped to recognise and to manage the conditions to ensure optimum collective learning.

2: Learning v. performing
Once it is acknowledged that failure is not only necessary for, but actually helps, learning, the relationship between learning and performance is recognised as complex. For learning to be optimal, a team must operate in an environment in which mistakes and performance failure are an accepted norm. Some learning must result in failure for further, deeper learning to occur.

3: Team type
There are different kinds of team. The specific needs and characteristics of the team need to be taken into account when identifying optimal circumstances for collective learning.

4: Team processes
Irrespective of whether a team's development processes occur in a progressive, cyclical, or non-sequential way, its ability to learn in a collective way will vary greatly at different points in the team's lifespan.

5: Team task
There are different kinds of task that a team has to carry out in order to meet the performance requirements of its work. The specific needs and characteristics of the task on which a team is working should be taken into account when identifying optimal circumstances for collective learning.

6: Organisational context
As teams operate within the wider context of organisations, the learning conditions established at an organisational level are likely to influence the way in which teams learn. It is important, therefore, that the organisation as a whole promotes a learning culture, strategy, structure and environment in order that collective team learning is not blocked at a higher level.

7: Team context
Contextual factors within a team or group itself impact on collective team learning and performance:

- A democratic, participative style of leadership, or even self-direction, leads to the highest levels of team innovation.
- Low group cohesiveness may be beneficial in the generation of creative ideas, and high group cohesiveness advantageous in their execution.
- Teams function most effectively when they consist of members who have a balanced set of diverse skills.

8: Individual skills
The skills which individuals bring with them into a team

environment can either facilitate or hinder collective learning and should therefore be taken into consideration during team development. More specifically, it is recognised that the following skills are necessary for effective team learning:

□ team, interactive, interpersonal and communication skills, such as providing others with accurate and complete information, changing position when others offer convincing data, handling conflict, and influencing others

□ action, problem-solving and decision-making skills, such as identifying improvement opportunities, and developing and selecting solutions

□ technical, functional or job skills, such as equipment operation and production processes.

9: Social context
A team's ability to learn in a collective way is influenced by the social context within which it operates:

□ Power differences between team members result in the exclusion of multiple perspectives. Optimal team learning therefore occurs when information and expertise are evenly distributed across the team.

□ Processes/activities which lead to the two-way flow of information across the team's boundaries are necessary if team learning is to occur.

□ Team members should develop a set of shared schema that enable them to think and act in new synergistic ways, with full co-ordination and a sense of unity.

□ Continual reflection on the results of actions is key if the team is to develop new knowledge.

10: Adoption of an integrated approach
The final and most important aspect in the generation of optimal conditions for team learning is the adoption of an integrated approach to the process. None of the above factors impacts on collective learning in isolation, and they should all therefore be taken into consideration when building/developing learning teams. Empowered team learning attempts to do just that, and in so doing outlines an optimal approach for achieving collective learning.

REFERENCES

ARGOTE L. *and* MCGRATH J. E. (1993) 'Group processes in organizations: continuity and change', in C. L. Cooper and I. T. Robertson (eds), *International Review of Industrial and Organizational Psychology*. Vol. 8. pp333–89. Chichester, John Wiley.

ARGOTE L., INSKO C. A., YOVETICH N. *and* ROMERO A. A. (1995) 'Group learning curves: the effects of turnover and task complexity on group performance'. *Journal of Applied Social Psychology*. Vol. 25. pp512–29.

ARGYRIS C. (1990) *Overcoming Organizational Defences: Facilitating organizational learning*. Boston, Allyn and Bacon.

BROOKS A. K. (1994) 'Power and the production of knowledge: collective team learning in work organizations'. *Human Resource Development Quarterly*. Vol. 5 (3). pp213–35. San Francisco, Calif., Jossey-Bass.

BUNKER B. *and* ALBAN B. (1997) *Large Group Interventions: Engaging the whole system for rapid change*. San Francisco, Calif., Jossey-Bass.

CAMPION M. A., PAPPER E. M. *and* MEDSKER G. J. (1996) 'Relations between work team characteristics and effectiveness: a replication and extension'. *Personnel Psychology*. Vol. 49. pp429–52.

CROSSAN M., DJURFELDT L., LANE H. W. *and* WHITE R. E. (1994) *Organizational Learning: Dimensions for a theory*. Western Business School Working Paper Series.

CUNNINGHAM I. (1994) *The Wisdom of Strategic Learning: The self-managed learning solution*. Maidenhead, McGraw-Hill.

DANAU D. *and* SOMMERLAD E. (1996) *Work-Based Learning: Thematic review of literature, case examples and networks*. Maastricht, the European Centre for Work and Society.

DECHANT K., MARSICK V. J. *and* KASL E. (1993) 'Towards a model of team learning'. *Studies in Continuing Education*. Vol. 15 (1). pp1–14.

DIXON N. (1994) *The Organizational Learning Cycle: How we can learn collectively*. Maidenhead, McGraw-Hill.

EMERY M. *and* PURSER R. (1996). *The Search Conference: A powerful method for planning organisational change and community action*. San Francisco, Calif., Jossey-Bass.

GLADSTEIN-ACONA D. (1987) 'Groups in organisations: extending laboratory models', in C. Hendrick (ed.), *Group Processes and Intergroup Relations*. London, Sage.

HACKMAN R. J. (1986) *Groups That Work (and Those That Don't): Creating conditions for effective teamwork*. San Francisco, Calif., Jossey-Bass.

JANIS I. L. (1982) *Groupthink*. Boston, Mass., Houghton Mifflin.

KATZENBACH J. R. *and* SMITH J. R. (1993). *The Wisdom of Teams: Creating the high-performing organisation*. Boston, Mass., Harvard Business School Press.

KING N. *and* ANDERSON N. (1990) 'Innovation and creativity in working groups', in M. A. West and J. Farr (eds), *Innovation and Creativity at Work*. Chichester, John Wiley.

KING N. *and* ANDERSON N. (1993) 'Innovation in organisations', in C. L. Cooper and I. T. Robertson (eds), *International Review of Industrial and Organisational Psychology*. Vol. 8. pp 1–34.

KNOWLES M. (1987) *The Adult Learner: A neglected species*. Houston, Tex., Gulf Publishing Company.

LEVINE J. M., RESNICK L. B. *and* HIGGINS E. T. (1993) 'Social foundations of cognition'. *Annual Review of Psychology*. Vol. 44. pp585–612.

McKENNA S. O. (1995) 'Moving a business forward through team learning', *Journal of Managerial Psychology*. Vol. 10. pp28–36.

MANZ C. C. *and* SIMS H. P. JR (1989) *Superleadership: Leading others to lead themselves*. Englewood Cliffs, N.J., Prentice-Hall.

PASCALE R. T. (1990) *Managing on the Edge*. London, Viking.

PEARN M. A. *and* MULROONEY C. (1995) *Tools for a Learning Organisation*. London, Institute of Personnel and Development.

PEARN M. A., MULROONEY C. *and* PAYNE T. (1998) *Ending the Blame Culture*. London, Gower.

PEARN M. A., RODERICK C. *and* MULROONEY C. (1995) *Learning Organizations in Practice*. Maidenhead, McGraw-Hill.

PEDLER M., BURGOYNE J. *and* BOYDELL T. (1988) *Learning*

Company Project Report. Sheffield, Manpower Services Commission.

PEDLER M., BURGOYNE J. *and* BOYDELL T. (1992) *The Learning Company: A strategy for sustainable development*. London, McGraw-Hill.

SCHEIN E. H. (1997) *Organisational Learning: What is new?* Society for Organisational Learning Working Papers.

SCHWANDT D. R. (1996) *Exploring Dynamic Organisational Learning Processes: A social action theory perspective*. ECLO 1996 Conference.

SEMLER R. (1993) *Maverick: The success story behind the world's most unusual workplace*. London, Century.

SENGE P. M., ROBERTS C., ROSS R. B., SMITH B. J. *and* KLEINER A. (1994) *The Fifth Discipline Fieldbook*. London, Nicholas Brealey.

SPARROW P. R. (1994) 'The psychology of strategic management: emerging themes of diversity and cognition', in C. L. Cooper and I. T. Robertson (eds), *International Review of Industrial and Organisational Psychology*. Vol. 9.

SPENCER L. J. (1989) *Winning through Participation*. Dubuque, IA., Kendall Hunt.

THOMSON C. J. C. *and* ZONDLO J. A. (1995) 'Building a case for team learning'. *Healthcare Forum Journal*. Vol. 38 (5). p36.

UNGAR H. *and* LORSCHEIDER B. (1996) *Groups: A neglected concept in organisational learning*. ECLO 1996 Conference.

WEISBORD M. *and* JANOFF S. (1995) *Future Search: An action guide to finding common ground in organisations and communities*. San Francisco, Calif., Berrett-Koehler.

WELLINS R. S., BYHAM W. C. *and* WILSON J. M. (1991) *Empowered Teams: Creating session lf-directed work groups that improve quality, productivity, and participation*. San Francisco, Calif., Jossey-Bass.

WEST M. A. *and* WALLACE M. (1988) 'Innovation in primary health care teams: the effects of roles and climate'. Paper presented at the Annual Occupational Psychology Conference of the British Psychological Society, University of Manchester.

INDEX

With over 90,000 members, the **Institute of Personnel and Development** is the largest organisation in Europe dealing with the management and development of people. The IPD operates its own publishing unit, producing books and research reports for human resource practitioners, students, and general managers charged with people management responsibilities.

Currently there are over 150 titles covering the full range of personnel and development issues. The books have been commissioned from leading experts in the field and are packed with the latest information and guidance to best practice.

For free copies of the IPD Books Catalogue, please contact the publishing department:

Tel.: 0181-263 3387
Fax: 0181-263 3850
E-mail: publish@ipd.co.uk
Web: http://www.ipd.co.uk

Orders for books should be sent to:

Plymbridge Distributors
Estover
Plymouth
Devon
PL6 7PZ

(Credit card orders) Tel.: 01752 202 301
Fax: 01752 202 333

NEW ADDITIONS TO THE *DEVELOPING PRACTICE* SERIES

Flexible Working Practices: Techniques and innovations
John Stredwick and Steve Ellis

Flexible working practices can make the difference between survival and success. Introducing flexible working practices can help organisations respond effectively to customer demand, cope with peaks and troughs in activity, recruit and retain the best people, and save significant sums of money. John Stredwick and Steve Ellis build on the experiences of leading-edge companies – from SmithKline Beecham to Siemens GEC, Birds Eye to Xerox, Cable and Wireless to the Co-operative Bank – to help practitioners develop effective policies on:

- temporal flexibility: annual hours, job sharing, part-time and portfolio working
- predicting the unpredictable: complementary workers, interim managers and new forms of shiftworking
- functional flexibility: multiskilling, outsourcing, tele-working and call centres
- using individual and team reward – competence-based, performance-based and profit-related pay, and gainsharing and broadbanding – to support flexibility
- 'family-friendly' policies: flexitime, career breaks, child-care and eldercare
- clarifying the 'psychological contract' with empowered employees.

A closing chapter pulls together the different options and sets out the main techniques for 'selling' flexibility to a sceptical workforce.

First edition
344 pages
Pbk
0 85292 744 4
1998
£18.95

Performance Management: The new realities
Angela Baron and Michael Armstrong

All employers need to find ways to improve the performance of their people. Yet many of today's personnel departments are abolishing rigid systems of performance management in favour of strategic frameworks that empower individual managers to communicate with, motivate and develop their staff. Here, one of Britain's best-known business writers and the IPD's policy adviser for employee resourcing draw on detailed data from over 550 organisations – including the latest innovations adopted by leading-edge companies, ranging from BP Exploration to the Corporation of London, and from AA Insurance to Zeneca – to illuminate how approaches to appraisal have evolved and to identify current best practice in performance management. They explore its history, philosophy and separate elements, the criticisms it has attracted and its impact (if any) on quantifiable business results. They also offer practitioners invaluable guidance on:

- the fundamental processes: from target-setting through measurement to performance and development reviews
- performance management skills: coaching, counselling and problem-solving
- meeting developmental needs and enhancing team performance
- paying for performance and competences
- introducing performance management and evaluating its effectiveness.

Throughout, the authors have tailored their suggestions to the practical problems revealed by their research. There could be no better source of support for organisations facing this most crucial challenge.

First edition
480 pages
Pbk
0 85292 727 4
1998
£18.95